Childhood Trauma and Recovery

Healing Your Inner Child

Contents

Introduction   1

1. Was it Even Abuse?   7

2. What's Happening Inside of Me?   12

3. Why Can't I "Just Get Over It"?   23

4. Why Do I Feel Stuck in the Same Relationship Patterns?   37

5. Why Do My Past Traumas Still Affect Me?   63

6. Who is My Inner Child and Why Do They Need Me?   87

7. How Can I Begin to Heal My Inner Child?   109

8. What Are Other Healing Techniques?   139

Conclusion   173

Appendix   177

Introduction

"The journey of a thousand miles begins with one step" – Lao Tzu

In a world where the wounds of the past often remain hidden, obscured by the hustle of daily life or the masks we wear to protect ourselves, the journey of healing from childhood trauma is both deeply personal and universally relevant. This book, "Childhood Trauma Recovery: Healing Your Inner Child," is not just a collection of professional insights and strategies; it is a symbol of hope, a guide for those who find themselves lost in the aftermath of early life experiences that have left indelible marks on their soul.

The essence of childhood trauma is complex and multifaceted. It can arise from experiences that are overtly abusive or subtly neglectful, from events that are singularly catastrophic or chronically stressful. The American Psychological Association defines trauma as an emotional response to a terrible event like an accident, rape, or natural disaster. However, this definition has expanded over the years to include the prolonged, repetitive stress of experiences like childhood neglect or abuse (American Psychological Association). These experiences, especially when unaddressed, can shape our personality, our relationships, and our view of the world in profound ways.

This book is designed to speak to you, whether you are a survivor of childhood trauma, a caregiver, a therapist, or simply someone who wishes to understand more about this critical aspect of human experience. Its structure, centered around key questions that frequently arise in the context of childhood trauma, is intended to offer both clarity and a sense of direction. Each chapter is crafted to address a specific aspect of childhood trauma, from understanding its roots to navigating the challenging path of recovery.

In writing this book, I have drawn upon a wealth of resources: the latest research in psychology and neuroscience, insights from therapy and counseling practices, and the powerful narratives of those who have walked the path of recovery. These sources collectively underscore the importance of a compassionate, informed approach to dealing with childhood trauma. For instance, a study by Dr. Nadine Burke Harris, a renowned pediatrician and trauma expert, highlights how adverse childhood experiences (ACEs) are linked to chronic health issues, mental illness, and substance misuse in adulthood (Harris, et al.). Such insights are pivotal in understanding the far-reaching impact of childhood t rauma.

As you embark on this journey through the pages of this book, remember that the road to healing is not linear. It is a path of discovery, of learning, and, most importantly, of reclaiming the narrative of your life. This book aims to be a companion in that journey, offering insights, tools, and most importantly, a message of hope: that healing is possible, and your inner child, no matter how wounded, can find a way back to peace and wh oleness.

CASE STUDY: NOELLE'S JOURNEY THROUGH THE SHADOWS

Noelle was in her mid-thirties when she first realized that the difficulties she faced in her adult life were deeply rooted in her childhood experiences. On the surface, Noelle was successful: a high-achieving professional with a stable job and a seemingly happy life. But beneath this veneer of success, she grappled with unexplained anxiety, a pervasive sense of unworthiness, and difficulties in forming close relationships.

Her journey of self-discovery began during a routine therapy session. It was there, in the safe confines of a therapist's office, that Noelle first spoke about her childhood. She described growing up in a home where her emotional needs were consistently ignored. Her parents, though not overtly abusive, were emotionally distant, preoccupied with their own issues, and often dismissive of her feelings.

Dr. Jonice Webb, a psychologist renowned for her work on Childhood

Emotional Neglect (CEN), states that this form of neglect, where a child's emotional needs are not adequately met, can have lasting negative effects on their adult life (Webb)). In Noelle's case, this neglect manifested in her constant search for validation and her struggles with self-esteem.

As therapy progressed, Noelle started to recognize patterns in her behavior that were linked to her childhood experiences. She often found herself overachieving, driven by a subconscious need to prove her worth. Her relationships were marked by a fear of abandonment, making her overly accommodating and reluctant to express her own needs.

A breakthrough came when Noelle learned about the concept of the 'inner child' – the part of one's psyche that retains the emotions, memories, and sensitivity of childhood. Renowned psychiatrist and author, Dr. Carl Jung, emphasized the importance of acknowledging and healing this part of oneself to achieve wholeness (Jung, 'The Archetypes and the Collective Unconscious). For Noelle, acknowledging her inner child meant understanding the deep-seated reasons behind her emotional responses and behaviors.

Through a combination of therapy, self-help exercises, and a supportive network, Noelle began the slow process of healing. She learned to nurture her inner child, to provide the validation and care that she had missed in her childhood. This was not a quick fix but a gradual journey of self-awareness and acceptance.

Noelle's story is not unique. It echoes the experiences of many who have faced childhood trauma in its various forms. Her journey is a testament to the resilience of the human spirit and the power of healing. It serves as a symbol of hope for others who embark on this challenging yet rewarding path towards recovery.

THE POWER OF QUESTIONS: A GUIDE TO OUR APPROACH

As you venture into the pages of "Childhood Trauma Recovery: Healing Your Inner Child," you'll notice that each chapter begins with a question. This isn't a stylistic choice made on a whim; rather, it's a deliberate strategy rooted in educational psychology and therapeutic practice, designed to engage you, the reader, on a deeper and more personal level.

- Engagement and Relatability: Questions naturally pique curiosity. According to a study published in the *Journal of Educational Psychology*, questions can stimulate cognitive engagement and enhance learning (Rosenshine). By framing each chapter around a question, the book aims to directly address the concerns that might be at the forefront of your mind or the minds of those affected by childhood trauma.

- Facilitating Self-Reflection: Questions encourage introspection. Dr. James Pennebaker, a psychologist renowned for his research on writing and healing, emphasizes the therapeutic power of writing and reflecting on personal experiences (Pennebaker, "Opening Up"). Each question in this book is designed to prompt you to reflect on your own experiences and feelings, fostering a deeper connection with the content.

- Guiding the Healing Journey: The journey of healing from childhood trauma is unique for each individual. The question-based format allows you to navigate this journey at your own pace, finding relevance and meaning in each chapter based on your personal history and current needs.

- Enhancing Clarity and Focus: The structure of question-based chapters brings clarity and focus to complex subjects. By breaking down the broad topic of childhood trauma into specific, manageable questions, the book aims to provide clear, focused insights into each aspect of trauma and recovery.

- Encouraging Active Learning: Active participation is crucial in the process of healing and personal growth. By engaging with the questions, you're not just passively receiving information; you're actively participating in your own process of understanding and healing.

- Building a Comprehensive Understanding: The cumulative effect of these questions is to build a holistic understanding of childhood trauma and its impact. Rather than presenting disjointed pieces of information, the question-based approach weaves a coherent narrative that encompasses the many facets of trauma and recovery.

In sum, the questions that headline each chapter are more than just titles; they are invitations to explore, understand, and heal. They are the guiding lights on a path that can often feel dark and uncertain. As you move through this book, let these questions be your companions, guiding you toward insights, healing, and, ultimately, a renewed sense of self.

Chapter Summary

- Defining Trauma: Childhood trauma includes both obvious and subtle experiences, deeply impacting emotional and physical health.

- Healing as a Journey: Emphasizes that recovering from trauma is a dynamic and personal process, involving self-discovery and growth.

- Illustrative Case Study: Noelle's story showcases the lasting impact of emotional neglect and the healing power of reconnecting with one's inner child.

Apply It!

Journal Prompts

1. Personal Expectations: What are my hopes and expectations from reading *Childhood Trauma and Recovery: Healing Your Inner Child*? What specific areas of my life do I wish to improve or understand better?

2. Reflecting on Childhood Experiences: Can I identify events or patterns from my childhood that may have impacted my adult life? How do I feel about these memories now?

3. Relating: How do you relate to Noelle's story of emotional neglect and her journey toward healing?

4. Understanding My Emotional Response: How do my childhood experiences influence my emotional responses in adulthood? Are there any recurring feelings or reactions that I can trace back to my early years?

Suggested Goals

1. Dedicated Reading and Reflection Time: Over the next two months, dedicate 30 minutes each day to reading *Childhood Trauma and Recovery: Healing Your Inner Child* and reflecting on its content. Choose a consistent time of day when you can read and reflect without distractions, aiming to deepen your understanding of the material and apply its teachings to your personal journey of healing and growth.

2. Journaling for Self-Discovery: For the duration of reading this book, commit to 15 minutes of journaling after each reading session. Focus on documenting your thoughts, feelings, and insights related to each chapter. Aim to complete at least one page per entry, using the journal as a reflective tool to track your emotional and cognitive journey through the book. By the end of your reading, aim to have a comprehensive journal that encapsulates your personal growth and learning.

3. Complete the exercises in the Introduction section of the *Childhood Trauma and Recovery Workbook* to deepen your understanding and apply the concepts discussed.

1

Was it Even Abuse?

UNRAVELING THE COMPLEXITIES OF CHILDHOOD TRAUMA

"You may not control all the events that happen to you, but you can decide not to be reduced by them." – Maya Angelou

I n this chapter, we'll explore a question that haunts many: "Was it even abuse?" The complexity of childhood trauma often leaves individuals questioning the validity of their experiences. This doubt can be a significant barrier to acknowledging the trauma and seeking help. Understanding childhood trauma is essential; it comes in various forms, not all of which are as overt or easily identifiable as physical abuse.

Childhood trauma encompasses a range of experiences, including emotional, physical, and sexual abuse, as well as neglect, which can be just as damaging as other forms of abuse. The Child Welfare Information Gateway describes neglect as a form of maltreatment that includes failing to provide necessary care, supervision, or affection (Child Welfare Information Gateway, 2019). Though less visible, neglect can have profound long-term effects on an individual's psychological and emotional development.

Moreover, the concept of childhood trauma extends beyond individual actions to include systemic issues and traumatic environments. The Substance Abuse and Mental Health Services Administration (SAMHSA) emphasizes the role of adverse community environments, such as violence and chronic poverty, in shaping childhood experiences (SAMHSA, 2014).

This chapter aims to broaden the understanding of what constitutes childhood trauma. By exploring various types and forms of trauma, we seek to validate the experiences of those who have suffered, often in silence. It's not just about the physical scars; it's about the emotional and psychological wounds that may not be visible to the eye but are deeply felt in the heart and mind.

As we journey through this chapter, we will examine the signs and symptoms of childhood trauma. The goal is to provide a compassionate understanding that empowers individuals to recognize and acknowledge their trauma. This recognition is the first step towards healing and reclaiming control over one's life story.

Exploring the Definition and Types of Trauma

Childhood trauma, a term encompassing a wide range of distressing experiences during one's formative years, profoundly impacts an individual's psychological, emotional, and physical well-being. The American Psychiatric Association defines trauma as an emotional response to a terrible event, such as an accident, war, or natural disaster. This definition has broadened to include chronic experiences like neglect, abuse, and living in a traumatic environment, as defined by the American Psychiatric Association (2013).

We will explore abuse as defined by the Adverse Childhood Experience (ACE) study, along with more subtle forms of abuse that often arise in what a particular therapist refers to as "Tricky Families" (Teahan).

The Ace Study and Questionnaire

The ACE Study, a landmark research project by the Centers for Disease Control and Prevention (CDC) and Kaiser Permanente, categorizes childhood trauma into three main groups:

1. Abuse (Physical, Emotional, Sexual)

2. Neglect (Physical, Emotional)

3. Household Challenges (Mental Illness, Incarceration, Substance Abuse, Parental Separation or Divorce)

Each type of adverse experience scores a point, revealing that a higher ACE score correlates with increased risks of negative health and social outcomes later in life.

The ACE Questionnaire, a critical element of the ACE Study, is a tool designed to identify and quantify these adverse childhood experiences. It asks respondents a series of questions about their exposure to various forms of abuse, neglect, and household dysfunction. The ACE Questionnaire is crucial in determining the potential impact of these experiences on long-term health and behavior. It aids professionals in understanding the complex interplay between early adverse experiences and adult health outcomes. Despite its significance, the ACE Questionnaire primarily focuses on overt forms of abuse and may not fully encompass the nuanced trauma encountered in subtly dysfunctional family environments.

INTRODUCING THE CONCEPT OF "TRICKY FAMILIES"

To address this gap, Patrick Teahan, LICSW, an expert in the field of childhood trauma, introduces the concept of "Tricky Families". These families might appear functional on the surface, providing basic needs and stability, yet they often fail to meet the children's emotional and developmental requirements. Characteristics of such families include emotionally unavailable parents, toxic intimacy dynamics, alcoholism, narcissistic or authoritarian attitudes, and environments where sharing external abuse experiences is unsafe. In "Tricky Families" the trauma may not be overt but can still significantly impact a child's development.

This subtler form of trauma, while aligning with the ACE Study categories, manifests in less obvious ways. Physical abuse might be in the form of spankings rather than beatings, emotional abuse might not involve explicit verbal assaults but could force a child into a parental role, and sexual abuse might include exposure to inappropriate materials. Similarly, domestic violence might be more verbal than physical.

Both blatant abuse and the insidious trauma of a "Tricky Family" can lead to long-term issues like intimacy problems, low self-esteem, depression, anxiety, addictions, attachment problems, and unhealthy reactions. Recognizing the spectrum of childhood experiences that lead to trauma is essential for understanding and addressing these experiences' long-term impacts.

CHAPTER SUMMARY

- The complexity of Childhood Trauma: Highlights the multifaceted nature of childhood trauma, including emotional, physical, and sexual abuse, as well as neglect.

- Trauma Beyond Physical Abuse: Explores how neglect and less visible forms of abuse significantly affect psychological and emotional development.

- Introduction of "Tricky Families" Concept: Patrick Teahan's concept explains how some families fail to meet emotional and developmental needs, leading to subtler forms of trauma.

- Long-Term Effects of Trauma: Discusses how both overt and subtle trauma can lead to issues like depression, anxiety, and relationship problems in adulthood.

- Encouraging Trauma Acknowledgment: Promotes the recognition and understanding of one's own childhood trauma as the first step towards healing and empowerment.

APPLY IT!

Journal Prompts

1. Reflecting on Emotional Neglect: Think about times in your childhood when your emotional needs might have been overlooked. How has this affected your adult relationships and self-esteem?

2. Identifying Subtle Trauma: Recall a situation from your childhood that seemed normal but may have been subtly traumatic. How do you perceive that event now?

3. Beyond the ACE Questionnaire: Consider an experience from your childhood that wouldn't typically be covered by the ACE Questionnaire but has had a significant impact on you.

4. "Tricky Families" Dynamics: Reflect on aspects of your family life that might fit the description of a "Tricky Family". How have these dynamics influenced your adult life?

Suggested Goals:

1. Acknowledgment Goal: Set a goal to acknowledge one aspect of your childhood trauma this week. It could be recognizing a pattern of emotional neglect or admitting the impact of a "Tricky Family" dynamic on your current behavior.

2. Self-Compassion Goal: Practice self-compassion by dedicating 10 minutes each day to affirm positive self-statements that counteract negative beliefs developed from childhood experiences.

3. Therapeutic Goal: If you haven't already, consider starting therapy or counseling focused on childhood trauma. Set a goal to research potential therapists or counseling services and make an initial appointment or consultation.

4. Complete the exercises in Chapter 1 of the *Childhood Trauma and Recovery Workbook* to deepen your understanding and apply the concepts discussed.

2

What's Happening Inside of Me?

DECIPHERING THE BODY AND BRAIN'S RESPONSE TO TRAUMA

"The conflict between the will to deny horrible events and the will to proclaim them aloud is the central dialectic of psychological trauma." – Judith Lewis Herman

The question, 'What's happening inside me?' is one many survivors of childhood trauma grapple with. Trauma, particularly when experienced in childhood, does not only leave emotional scars; it can also lead to significant and sometimes lasting changes in both the body and the brain. This chapter looks into the intricate ways trauma can alter our physical and neurological states, often in ways invisible to the eye but deeply felt within.

The understanding of how trauma affects the body and brain has evolved significantly over the years. Advances in neuroscience and psychophysiology have illuminated the tangible changes that occur in response to traumatic experiences. These changes are not merely psychological symptoms but are embedded in the very structures and functions of our bodies and brains.

Physically, trauma can manifest in various ways, from heightened stress responses and changes in the immune system to an increased risk of chronic health conditions. The American Psychological Association reports that prolonged stress, like that experienced in childhood trauma, can lead to physical health problems, including heart disease, diabetes, and autoimmune disorders (American Psychological Association).

Neurologically, trauma can leave its mark on the brain, affecting areas that regulate emotion, memory, and executive functioning. Groundbreaking research has shown that exposure to trauma, especially in childhood, can alter the structure and functioning of the brain, impacting the amygdala, hippocampus, and prefrontal cortex (Teicher, *The Journal of Neuropsychiatry and Clinical Neurosciences*). These changes can influence everything from emotional regulation to memory processing and decision-making.

In this chapter, we will explore the various physical and brain effects of trauma, examining the latest research and understanding of these phenomena. We aim to provide insights into the often-overlooked physical dimensions of trauma, explaining how and why the body and brain react as they do, and what this means for those living with the legacy of traumatic experiences.

Understanding the physical and neurological impacts of trauma is crucial, not only for survivors but also for healthcare providers, therapists, and loved ones supporting them. It offers a more comprehensive view of trauma's effects, paving the way for more effective treatment and healing strategies that address both the mind and the body.

HOW TRAUMA AFFECTS BRAIN DEVELOPMENT AND FUNCTION

The impact of trauma, especially in childhood, extends deeply into the realm of brain development and function. Trauma during these formative years can lead to significant and sometimes lasting changes in the brain, affecting an individual's emotional, cognitive, and social functioning. This subchapter explores the specific ways in which trauma alters brain development and function, drawing on current neuroscience research and expert analysis.

CHANGES IN BRAIN STRUCTURE AND VOLUME

Research has demonstrated that trauma can lead to changes in the size and volume of specific brain areas. The amygdala, a critical region involved in emotional processing and fear response, is often profoundly affected by trauma.

J.D. Bremner's work, as published in *Neuropsychopharmacology*, reveals that individuals with a history of trauma may exhibit an enlarged and hyperactive amygdala. This hyperactivity is associated with increased vigilance and sensitivity to stress, often leading to heightened responses to perceived threats.

Such changes represent the brain's adaptive mechanisms for survival, enhancing an individual's ability to detect and respond to danger, though this comes at the cost of increased anxiety and stress sensitivity.

Conversely, the hippocampus, essential for memory and learning, frequently displays a reduction in volume following traumatic experiences. This decrease in size can significantly affect memory processing and stress regulation. The loss of hippocampal volume is associated with difficulties in forming new memories and managing stress. This change has been observed in various populations, including trauma survivors and military veterans with PTSD, in studies conducted by Bremner and others.

Understanding these changes in brain structure and volume is crucial for developing effective treatment strategies for trauma survivors. Therapies focused on regulating the body's stress response, such as mindfulness and relaxation techniques, can be particularly beneficial in managing amygdala hyperactivity. Similarly, interventions targeting memory processing and cognitive rehabilitation can provide support for individuals experiencing hippocampal volume loss.

ALTERED STRESS RESPONSE SYSTEMS

The impact of trauma on the body's stress response system, particularly the hypothalamic-pituitary-adrenal (HPA) axis, is one of its most profound effects. This alteration is especially evident in children who have experienced trauma and can have lasting implications on these health and stress management.

The HPA axis is a central part of the body's stress response system. When a person experiences a traumatic event, this axis is stimulated to release stress hormones, primarily cortisol. This response is crucial for handling immediate stressors. However, in the case of trauma, especially repeated or chronic trauma, this system can become dysregulated. The continuous activation of the HPA axis leads to consistently high levels of cortisol and other stress hormones in the bloodstream.

In their 2006 study published in *Developmental Psychobiology*, Tarullo and Gunner explore how this overactivity manifests. They found that children with a history of trauma often exhibit a heightened and prolonged HPA axis response to stress. This heightened response was not only in reaction to traumatic reminders but also to everyday stressors, indicating a fundamental shift in the stress response system.

The persistently high levels of cortisol can disrupt various bodily functions. Cortisol, known as the 'stress hormone' plays a role in numerous physiological processes, including metabolism, immune response, and inflammatory pathways. Chronic overexposure to cortisol can lead to metabolic imbalances, reduced immune function, and increased inflammation. These conditions are risk factors for various health issues such as obesity, diabetes, autoimmune diseases, and cardiovascular problems.

Beyond physical health, an overactive HPA axis impacts mental health and cognitive functions. Elevated cortisol levels have been linked to mood disorders such as anxiety and depression. Cognitive functions, particularly memory and executive functioning can also be affected. Prolonged exposure to high cortisol levels can impair the consolidation of new memories and reduce cognitive flexibility, leading to difficulties in learning and decision-making.

The insights from Tarulb and Gunnar's research have broader implications for understanding and treating trauma. They suggest the necessity of interventions that target the physiological aspects of trauma, such as stress management techniques, mindfulness practices, and, in some cases, medication to regulate the stress response. The interventions can help in rebalancing the HPA axis thereby mitigating the long term health risks associated with its overactivity.

IMPACT OF TRAUMA ON EMOTIONAL REGULATION AND THE PREFRONTAL CORTEX

The prefrontal cortex is instrumental in higher-order cognitive processes. It helps in planning, reasoning, problem-solving, and regulating emotions. This part of the brain acts like a control center, managing both thoughts and feelings, particularly in stressful situations. It's involved in the inhibition of impulsive responses and the consideration of the consequences of actions.

When an individual experiences trauma, the functioning of the prefrontal cortex can be altered. Research has shown that traumatic stress can impair the development and functioning of this brain region. This impairment can lead to difficulties in controlling emotions and behaviors. Trauma survivors might find it harder to manage anger, anxiety, sadness, or other intense emotions. This can manifest as mood swings, emotional outbursts, or heightened emotional sensitivity.

Alongside emotional dysregulation, trauma can affect an individual's ability to make decisions and control impulsive behaviors. The prefrontal cortex is crucial for evaluating the long-term consequences of actions and for making reasoned decisions. When this area is impacted by trauma, individuals may exhibit increased impulsivity, poor judgment, and difficulty in planning and organizing.

The changes in emotional regulation and decision-making directly affect one's ability to form and maintain healthy relationships. The inability to regulate emotions can lead to conflict, miscommunication, and difficulties in forming close, trusting relationships. In more severe cases, it can contribute to the development of relationship patterns that are either overly dependent or detached.

The long-term consequences of these changes can be significant. However, it's important to note that the brain has a remarkable capacity for adaptation and healing. Therapeutic interventions, such as cognitive-behavioral therapy, mindfulness-based therapies, and emotional regulation strategies, can help retrain and strengthen the prefrontal cortex's functioning. These therapies can aid trauma survivors in developing healthier ways to manage emotions and impulses, ultimately improving their decision-making and relationship-building skills.

DEVELOPMENTAL TIMING OF TRAUMA: ITS IMPACT ON BRAIN DEVELOPMENT AND FUNCTIONING

The brain's vulnerability to trauma varies based on the developmental stage at which the trauma occurs. For instance, trauma during a period of rapid brain development, such as early childhood or adolescence, can have more pronounced effects compared to other stages. Each stage of development has specific neural and psychological milestones, and trauma can disrupt the achievement of these milestones.

Trauma experienced during early childhood, particularly in the first few years of life, can have profound effects on the brain's development. This period is critical for the formation of secure attachments and the development of basic trust. Trauma during this stage, such as neglect or abuse, can disrupt the development of the attachment system, leading to difficulties in forming secure relationships later in life. It can also impact the development of brain regions involved in stress regulation, such as the HPA axis, leading to increased vulnerability to stress and anxiety.

Trauma experienced during middle childhood and adolescence can significantly disrupt the key developmental tasks characteristic of these stages. These include the formation of a sense of self, the development of autonomy, and the acquisition of social skills. It is during these critical periods that the brain undergoes substantial changes in areas governing executive functioning, decision-making, and social cognition. When trauma occurs, it can interfere with the development of these critical brain regions. This interference can result in challenges related to executive functions and problem-solving skills, as well as difficulties in social interactions. Additionally, adolescents who experience trauma face a heightened risk of developing mental health issues, such as depression and anxiety disorders. In adolescence, specifically, trauma may be more intricately linked with identity formation, engagement in risk-taking behaviors, and the establishment of social relationships.

Understanding the developmental timing of trauma is crucial for providing effective support and treatment. Interventions need to be tailored to address the specific developmental challenges posed by trauma at different stages. For instance, early childhood trauma might require interventions focused on building secure attachments and emotional regulation, while trauma during adolescence might necessitate a focus on identity development, social skills, and coping strategies.

SOCIOEMOTIONAL DEVELOPMENT

One of the key aspects of socioemotional development is the ability to accurately recognize and interpret social cues, such as facial expressions, body language, and tone of voice. Trauma can disrupt this ability, making it challenging for individuals to read and respond appropriately to social signals. This difficulty can stem from a heightened state of alertness or distrust, as well as from altered brain development in areas responsible for processing social information.

Empathy, the ability to understand and share the feelings of others, can also be affected by trauma. Traumatic experiences, particularly those involving relational trauma or emotional abuse, can lead to difficulties in empathizing with others. This can result from a need to protect oneself emotionally, or from disruptions in the development of brain regions involved in understanding emotions.

Secure attachment, the deep and enduring emotional bond that develops between a child and caregiver, is crucial for healthy socio-emotional development. Trauma, especially when it involves primary caregivers or occurs in early childhood, can lead to attachment issues. Individuals with a history of trauma may struggle with trust, intimacy, and dependency, manifesting in insecure or disorganized attachment styles. This can impact their relationships throughout life, making it difficult to form close, stable connections.

The cumulative effect of these challenges in social cue recognition, empathy, and attachment can significantly hinder an individual's ability to engage in healthy social interactions. They may struggle with making and maintaining friendships, experience social isolation, or have difficulty in romantic relationships. The lack of supportive and stable relationships can further exacerbate feelings of loneliness and misunderstanding, creating a cycle that can be hard to break.

Addressing these socioemotional challenges requires targeted interventions. Social skills training, therapy focused on attachment and relationships, and interventions aimed at building empathy and emotional understanding are crucial. Such therapies not only address the symptoms but also work towards healing the underlying trauma, helping individuals to develop the skills and resilience needed for healthy social and emotional functioning.

Understanding the ways in which trauma affects brain development and function is crucial for developing effective treatment and support strategies for trauma survivors. It also offers hope, highlighting the brain's remarkable ability to adapt and heal. This subchapter not only sheds light on the neurological impact of trauma but also emphasizes the importance of early intervention and the potential for recovery and healing.

THE BODY'S RESPONSE TO TRAUMATIC

EXPERIENCES

The impact of trauma is not confined to the mind; it also manifests profoundly within the body. The body's response to traumatic experiences is complex, involving a range of physiological and biochemical changes. This subchapter examines these responses, providing insight into how trauma can leave a lasting imprint on the body.

FIGHT, FLIGHT, FREEZE, AND FAWN RESPONSES

One of the most immediate responses to trauma is the activation of the body's survival mechanisms, often characterized by fight, flight, freeze, and fawn responses.

These are mediated by the sympathetic nervous system and involve a surge of adrenaline and cortisol. The fight-or-flight response prepares the body to either confront or flee from the threat. The freeze response, on the other hand, involves a state of immobility and numbness, akin to 'playing dead,' as a defense mechanism. The fawn response, a less commonly known reaction, entails a tendency to appease or please the threat in an attempt to avoid further conflict or harm.

While these responses are crucial for survival, prolonged activation due to chronic or repeated trauma can lead to an array of health problems. For example, constant fight-or-flight stimulation can result in hypertension and weakened immune function, while the freeze response can contribute to dissociative symptoms and emotional numbing. Understanding the body's multifaceted response to trauma is essential for comprehensive treatment and healing.

CHANGES IN THE STRESS HORMONE SYSTEM

As previously mentioned, repeated activation of the HPA axis can disrupt its normal functioning, leading to imbalances in cortisol levels. This dysregulation can contribute to various health issues, including anxiety disorders, depression, and chronic fatigue syndrome.

THE ROLE OF THE AUTONOMIC NERVOUS SYSTEM AND SOMATIC SYMPTOMS IN TRAUMA

Trauma can lead to a dysregulation of the ANS, which controls involuntary bodily functions like heart rate, digestion, and breathing.

This dysregulation can manifest in two primary ways: hyperarousal (heightened alertness and sensitivity to stimuli) and hyperarousal (numbness and disconnection).

When the sympathetic branch of the ANS is overactive (hyperarousal), individuals may experience a range of somatic symptoms. These can include increased heart rate, hypertension, rapid breathing, muscle tension, and gastrointestinal issues. These symptoms are the body's natural response to perceived threats but can become chronic in the aftermath of trauma.

In contrast, when the parasympathetic branch becomes overactive (hypoarousal), it can lead to a 'shutdown' state. This state might manifest physically as fatigue, lethargy, slowed heart rate, digestive issues, and a general sense of physical detachment or numbness.

Long-term dysregulation of the ANS and the associated symptoms can have significant health implications. Chronic stress responses can contribute to a range of health issues, including cardiovascular disease, gastrointestinal disease, and chronic pain conditions.

Addressing these issues often involves therapies aimed at regulating the ANS. This might include mindfulness practices, biofeedback, somatic experiences, and other body-centered therapies. These approaches can help individuals gain better control over their physiological responses, alleviating somatic symptoms and improving overall well-being.

CHAPTER SUMMARY

- Trauma's Profound Impact: Trauma, particularly from childhood, leads to both emotional scars and significant changes in the body and brain.

- Neurological Alterations: Traumatic experiences can change the brain's structure and function, particularly in areas controlling emotion, memory, and executive function.

- Physical Manifestation: Trauma can result in heightened stress responses, changes in the immune system, and an increased risk of chronic health conditions.

- Comprehensive Understanding: A deep understanding of trauma's physical and neurological impacts is vital for effective treatment and overall healing.

- Hope in Adaptation and Healing: The chapter highlights the brain's capacity for adaptation and recovery, emphasizing the potential for healing from trauma.

APPLY IT!

Journal Prompts

1. Connecting Physical Symptoms to Trauma: Reflect on any physical symptoms you've experienced that may be connected to past trauma. Write about these symptoms and how they might relate to your stress response (fight, flight, freeze, or fawn).

2. Brain Changes and Trauma Impact: Consider the changes in the brain caused by trauma, such as alterations in the amygdala or hippocampus. Journal about how these changes might manifest in your daily life, especially in how you process emotions or memories.

3. Stress Reactions and Past Trauma: Write about a time when you experienced heightened stress or anxiety. Do you see a connection between this reaction and your past traumatic experiences? How does this understanding help you in managing these responses?

4. Trauma-Influenced Decision-Making: Think about how trauma has affected your decision-making or emotional regulation. Identify specific instances and reflect on how these might be linked to neurological changes from your trauma.

5. Trauma's Physical Echo: Reflect on the concept of the body keeping the score of trauma. Write about any physical sensations or reactions you have that might be a response to past trauma.

Suggested Goals

1. Mind-Body Connection Goal: Practice a mind-body technique (like mindfulness, yoga, or deep breathing) daily for a month to

help regulate the body's stress response systems.

2. Self-Awareness Goal: Spend 15 minutes each day journaling about your physical and emotional responses to everyday stressors, helping to build awareness of your body's trauma responses.

3. Health Check Goal: Schedule a comprehensive health examination to explore any potential physical health issues related to prolonged stress or trauma, and discuss these concerns with your healthcare provider.

4. Complete the exercises in Chapter 2 of the *Childhood Trauma and Recovery Workbook* to deepen your understanding and apply the concepts discussed.

3

Why Can't I "Just Get Over It"?

UNRAVELING THE PERSISTENT ECHOES OF CHILDHOOD TRAUMA

"Trauma is not what happens to you, but what happens inside you as a result of what happens to you." – Gabor Mate

In the preceding chapter, we explored the immediate and profound changes that occur in the brain and body as a result of childhood trauma. We explored how trauma in the formative years can reshape neural pathways, alter stress responses, and leave indelible marks on an individual's psychological and physical well-being. Building on this foundation, Chapter 3, "Why Can't I Just Get Over It?", shifts our focus to the enduring legacy of these early experiences.

This chapter seeks to answer a question that echoes in the minds of many survivors: Why, despite time and distance from these events, do the shadows of childhood trauma linger so persistently in adulthood? Here, we explore the long-term effects of childhood trauma, extending beyond the initial neurological and physiological responses. We examine how these early traumatic experiences continue to manifest in various aspects of adult life, influencing mental health, physical well-being, and daily functioning.

We will unravel the complex tapestry of adulthood depression, bipolar disorder, and various anxiety disorders, revealing how they are intricately woven with threads of past trauma. The journey continues through the intricate corridors of PTSD and C-PTSD, where the past's echoes are not just memories but lived realities. The path leads us to confront the challenges of addiction and substance abuse, often intertwined with attempts to silence the pain of traumatic memories.

Our exploration delves into the realm of chronic pain and how the body remembers what the mind strives to forget. We look at the far-reaching impacts on cardiovascular and respiratory health, unveiling the systemic nature of trauma's legacy. Finally, we address the often-overlooked but significant issues of hoarding and Attention Deficit Hyperactivity Disorder (ADHD), offering insights into their potential roots in a troubled past.

Chapter 3 is more than an exposition of conditions; it's an empathetic journey into the why behind these long-lasting effects. It seeks to provide understanding, validation, and a framework for recognizing how the echoes of childhood trauma reverberate throughout life. By understanding these enduring impacts, we aim not only to acknowledge the depth of these challenges but also to open pathways toward healing and resilience.

DEPRESSION

In the context of someone who has experienced childhood trauma, depression is a mood disorder characterized by pervasive sadness, loss of interest in activities, and feelings of worthlessness or hopelessness. These symptoms are more profound and persistent than the normal, temporary emotional responses to daily challenges and events.

Childhood trauma contributes to depression in adults in several ways:

- Altered Brain Development: Childhood trauma can cause changes in brain areas like the hippocampus and prefrontal cortex, crucial for mood regulation and stress response, making individuals more prone to depression.

- Psychological Impact: Trauma leads to negative self-perception, low self-esteem, and maladaptive coping strategies, which are significant risk factors for adult depression.

- Hormonal Imbalances: Trauma can disrupt stress hormone levels, such as cortisol, affecting mood regulation and increasing the likelihood of depression.

- Attachment Issues: Early trauma can impair the ability to form secure attachments, a protective factor against depression, leading to difficulties in relationships and trust.

- Emotional Scars: The unresolved emotional burden from childhood trauma, such as prolonged sadness and helplessness, can contribute to the development of depression in adulthood.

BIPOLAR DISORDER

Bipolar Disorder is a mental health condition characterized by extreme mood swings that include emotional highs (mania or hypomania) and lows (depression). During a manic phase, an individual might feel overly happy, energetic, or unusually irritable, while the depressive phase brings about feelings of sadness, hopelessness, and a loss of interest in most activities. These mood swings can affect sleep, energy, activity, judgment, behavior, and the ability to think clearly.

How childhood trauma contributes to bipolar disorder in adults:

- Emotional Regulation Disruption: Trauma can impair the development of brain regions involved in emotional regulation, increasing susceptibility to mood swings.

- Stress Response Alteration: Childhood trauma can lead to dysfunctional stress response systems, contributing to the heightened emotional states seen in bipolar disorder.

- Developmental Impact: Traumatic experiences during formative years can disrupt normal psychological development, potentially leading to bipolar disorder symptoms.

- Attachment and Self-Image Issues: Trauma can affect attachment styles and self-perception factors that are linked to the onset of bipolar disorder.

- Coping Mechanisms: Trauma survivors might develop maladaptive coping strategies that can manifest as symptoms of bipolar disorder.

ANXIETY

Anxiety, in a general sense, refers to intense, excessive, and persistent worry and fear about everyday situations. It often involves repeated episodes of sudden feelings of intense anxiety and fear or terror that reach a peak within minutes (panic attacks). These feelings of anxiety and panic interfere with daily activities, are difficult to control, are out of proportion to the actual danger, and can last a long time.

The ways childhood trauma contributes to anxiety in adults:

- Heightened Stress Response: Trauma can sensitize the body's stress response, leading to an exaggerated anxiety reaction to perceived threats.

- Altered Brain Function: Trauma impacts brain areas involved in fear and stress management, such as the amygdala, increasing vulnerability to anxiety.

- Persistent Fear and Hypervigilance: Traumatic experiences can instill a long-lasting sense of fear and hypervigilance, characteristic of anxiety disorders.

- Trust and Safety Issues: Childhood trauma can disrupt the sense of safety and trust, contributing to feelings of anxiety and insecurity in adulthood.

- Emotional Regulation Difficulties: Trauma can impair the ability to regulate emotions, leading to increased anxiety responses to stressors.

POST-TRAUMATIC STRESS DISORDER (PTSD)

Post-Traumatic Stress Disorder (PTSD) is a mental health condition triggered by a terrifying event, either experiencing it or witnessing it. Symptoms may include flashbacks, nightmares, severe anxiety, and uncontrollable thoughts about the event. People with PTSD may feel stressed or frightened even when they are not in danger.

How childhood trauma contributes to PTSD in adults:

- Traumatic Memories: Childhood trauma can result in lasting, distressing memories and flashbacks, central to PTSD.

- Hyperarousal: Trauma can lead to a heightened state of

physiological arousal, contributing to the anxiety and stress characteristic of PTSD.

- Emotional Numbing: Trauma survivors may develop emotional numbness as a coping mechanism, a common symptom of PTSD.

- Avoidance Behavior: Trauma can cause avoidance of reminders of the trauma, a key feature of PTSD.

- Trust and Safety Disruption: Childhood trauma often disrupts a sense of safety and trust, leading to fear and hypervigilance seen in PTSD.

COMPLEX POST-TRAUMATIC STRESS DISORDER (C-PTSD)

Complex Post-Traumatic Stress Disorder (C-PTSD) is a psychological disorder that can develop due to prolonged, repeated experiences of interpersonal trauma in a context in which the individual has little or no chance of escape. C-PTSD involves complex and severe psychological harm, often with long-term impacts.

How childhood trauma contributes to C-PTSD in adults:

- Prolonged Traumatic Experiences: Continuous and repeated trauma during childhood significantly increases the risk of developing C-PTSD.

- Impaired Emotional Regulation: Extended exposure to traumatic events can severely disrupt emotional regulation, a core aspect of C-PTSD.

- Deep Rooted Trust Issues: Persistent childhood trauma often leads to profound trust issues and relational difficulties, characteristic of C-PTSD.

- Persistent Negative Self-Perception: Continuous trauma can ingrain feelings of helplessness, guilt, and shame, contributing to the negative self-perception seen in C-PTSD.

- Complex Psychological Impact: The multifaceted nature of sustained trauma in childhood contributes to the complex symptomatology of C-PTSD, including difficulties in relationships, emotional stability, and self-identity.

CHRONIC PAIN RELATED DISORDERS

Chronic pain-related disorders encompass a range of conditions where individuals experience persistent pain that lasts for weeks, months, or even years. This category includes conditions like Chronic Pain Syndrome and Fibromyalgia, where pain is a prominent symptom. In these conditions, pain persists beyond the usual course of an acute illness or injury, and may not be associated with an ongoing cause. Chronic pain can significantly impact an individual's quality of life, affecting physical abilities, emotional states, and social relationships.

Chronic pain-related disorders in adults are often linked to experiences of childhood trauma, such as abuse, neglect, or prolonged stress and contributes to chronic pain related disorders in the following ways:

- Heightened Pain Sensitivity: Trauma can increase the body's sensitivity to pain, a phenomenon known as central sensitization.

- Immune System Dysregulation: Childhood trauma can disrupt the immune system, contributing to inflammation and autoimmune conditions that cause chronic pain.

- Psychological Impact: The emotional and psychological stress from trauma can amplify the perception and severity of pain.

- Stress Response Dysregulation: Trauma can lead to a dysregulated stress response system, exacerbating pain-related disorders.

- Behavioral Factors: Trauma survivors might develop behaviors (e.g., physical inactivity) that increase the risk of chronic pain conditions.

EATING DISORDERS

Eating disorders, such as anorexia nervosa, bulimia nervosa, and binge eating disorder, often have a significant link to childhood trauma. These eating disorders are characterized by severe food restriction leading to emaciation (anorexia nervosa), and cycles of binge eating followed by purging behaviors (bulimia nervosa). Trauma can affect an individual's relationship with food and body image in profound ways.

- Control and Coping Mechanisms: Trauma survivors may use

eating behaviors as a means to exert control or cope with emotional distress.

- Body Image Issues: Childhood trauma can lead to negative body image and self-esteem issues, contributing to eating disorders.

- Emotional Dysregulation: Trauma can result in difficulties regulating emotions, sometimes expressed through disordered eating.

- Neurobiological Changes: Trauma can impact brain regions related to reward and stress, influencing eating behaviors.

- Attachment and Trust Issues: Traumatic experiences, especially involving caregivers, can disrupt healthy eating patterns and attitudes toward food.

BORDERLINE PERSONALITY DISORDER

Borderline Personality Disorder (BPD) is often linked to childhood trauma. It is characterized by persistent patterns of mood instability, impulsivity, difficulty with interpersonal relationships, self-image issues, and intense, often unpredictable, emotional responses. Trauma, especially when it involves neglect, abuse, or unstable family environments, can significantly contribute to the development of BPD.

- Emotional Regulation Difficulties: Trauma can impair emotional regulation, a key issue in BPD.

- Unstable Relationships: Early trauma can lead to difficulties in forming stable, healthy relationships.

- Fear of Abandonment: Trauma, particularly involving caregivers, can instill a deep fear of abandonment, common in BPD.

- Impulsivity and Risky Behaviors: Truma can increase impulsivity and engagement in risky behaviors.

- Identity Disturbances: Truma may contribute to persistent identity disturbances seen in BPD.

CARDIO AND CIRCULATORY DISORDERS

Cardio and circulatory disorders refer to a range of conditions affecting the heart and blood vessels. these disorders include heart disease, hypertension (high blood pressure), and stroke. They can impact the body's ability to circulate blood effectively leading to various health complications.

How childhood trauma contributes to cardio and circulatory disorders:

- Chronic Stress Response: Trauma can cause a long-term activation of the body's stress response, leading to cardiovascular strain.

- Inflammatory Response: Childhood trauma is linked to increased inflammation, a risk factor for heart disease.

- Behavioral Factors: Trauma survivors may adopt unhealthy habits (e.g., smoking, poor diet) that increase cardiovascular risk.

- Psychological Impact: The stress and anxiety associated with trauma can contribute to hypertension and other heart problems.

- Altered Physiological Responses: Trauma can affect heart rate and blood pressure regulation, increasing the risk of circulatory disorders.

RESPIRATORY DISORDERS

Respiratory disorders in the context of childhood trauma encompass various conditions that affect breathing and lung function, such as asthma and frequent respiratory infections. These disorders can be exacerbated or influenced by early traumatic experiences.

How childhood trauma contributes to respiratory disorders:

- Immune System Dysregulation: Trauma can lead to an impaired immune response, making individuals more susceptible to respiratory infections.

- Stress Response: Chronic stress from trauma can affect respiratory function and exacerbate conditions like asthma.

- Behavioral Factors: Trauma survivors may adopt habits (e.g., smoking) that negatively impact respiratory health.

- Psychological Stress: Anxiety and emotional distress associated with trauma can trigger or worsen respiratory symptoms.

- Autonomic Nervous System Impact: Trauma can influence the autonomic nervous system, which regulates breathing, potentially leading to respiratory issues.

SYSTEMIC AND LONG-TERM HEALTH CONSEQUENCES

Childhood trauma's systemic and long-term health consequences are broad and can significantly impact an individual's overall well-being. These consequences go beyond immediate psychological effects, influencing various bodily systems. The implications can manifest in diverse ways, ranging from autoimmune diseases (such as Rheumatoid Arthritis, Lupus, Multiple Sclerosis, and Type 1 Diabetes) to accelerated aging (Telomere shortening), and can affect multiple organ systems, reflecting the profound and lasting impact of early adverse experiences.

How childhood trauma contributes to systemic and long-term health consequences:

- Immune System Alteration: Trauma can lead to changes in the immune system, increasing susceptibility to autoimmune diseases.

- Chronic Inflammation: Prolonged stress responses from trauma can cause systemic inflammation, contributing to various health issues.

- Accelerated Cellular Aging: Traumatic stress can accelerate aging at a cellular level, indicated by shortened telomeres.

- Hormonal Imbalances: Trauma can disrupt hormonal systems, affecting long-term health.

- Behavioral Factors: Traumatic experiences often lead to unhealthy behaviors (e.g., smoking, poor diet) that can worsen long-term health outcomes.

POSSIBLE LINKS TO CHILDHOOD TRAUMA

ATTENTION DEFICIT HYPERACTIVITY DISORDER

(ADHD)

Attention Deficit Hyperactivity Disorder is a neurodevelopmental disorder characterized by persistent patterns of inattention, hyperactivity, and impulsivity that can interfere with daily functioning and development. The study titled *Childhood Trauma and ADHD – Association or Diagnostic Confusion? A Clinical Perspective*, published in the journal *Attention Deficit and Hyperactivity Disorders* in 2020, provides an insightful analysis of the correlation between childhood trauma and adult ADHD. It focuses on exploring the overlap between the symptoms of ADHD and the long-term effects of childhood trauma. The research involved a clinical examination of adult patients diagnosed with ADHD, assessing their symptoms in light of their childhood trauma experiences. The findings indicate a significant link between traumatic experiences in childhood and the manifestation of ADHD symptoms in adults. The study highlights the complexity of differentiating between symptoms arising from ADHD and those resulting from historical trauma, emphasizing the importance of considering a patient's trauma history in the diagnosis process. This research underscores the need for a nuanced approach in the treatment and assessment of ADHD in adults, acknowledging the potential impact of early life trauma on their symptoms.

NARCISSISTIC PERSONALITY DISORDER (NPD)

Narcissistic Personality Disorder is a mental health condition characterized by a pervasive pattern of grandiosity, a constant need for admiration, and a lack of empathy for others. People with NPD often have an exaggerated sense of self-importance, believe they are unique or special, require excessive admiration, and have a sense of entitlement. They can be manipulative in their relationships and have difficulty maintaining healthy and empathetic connections with others.

Research into the link between childhood trauma and the development of Narcissistic Personality Disorder (NPD) in adulthood indicates a complex relationship. Studies have shown that certain forms of childhood trauma, such as emotional abuse, neglect, or excessively permissive parenting, may be associated with the development of narcissistic traits. However, the relationship is not universally established and can vary based on individual experiences and other contributing factors.

Childhood trauma can influence the development of self-esteem, empathy, and emotional regulation, which are key aspects affected by NPD. The neurobiological impact of trauma, particularly on brain areas involved in empathy and emotional regulation, could potentially contribute to the development of narcissistic behaviors. However, the neurobiological underpinnings in the context of NPD are less clearly defined compared to other personality disorders.

From a psychological perspective, childhood trauma can lead to coping mechanisms that may manifest as narcissistic traits. For example, a child who experiences emotional abuse or neglect may develop an inflated sense of self or entitlement as a defense mechanism. Similarly, inconsistent or overly idealizing parenting may lead to an unrealistic self-image and difficulty with empathy and intimacy. These psychological adaptations can contribute to the development of narcissistic personality traits, although they do not necessarily result in full-blown NPD.

HOARDING

Hoarding is a complex mental health disorder characterized by the excessive accumulation and retention of items, often ones that are considered to be of little or no value. The study titled *Childhood Trauma and Hoarding Behavior in Adults* published in the *Journal of Psychological Disorders*, sheds light on the relationship between childhood trauma and hoarding tendencies in adulthood. This research examined a sample of adults with hoarding disorder and explored their histories of childhood trauma, including experiences of emotional abuse, neglect, and adverse childhood events. The findings indicated a significant association between childhood trauma and the development of hoarding behaviors in adulthood. Individuals with a history of such trauma were more likely to exhibit hoarding symptoms, and the severity of their hoarding tendencies was positively correlated with the degree of childhood trauma experienced.

Dr. Randy O. Frost, renowned for his extensive research on hoarding behavior, has significantly contributed to understanding its complexities, including potential links to childhood trauma. His work primarily examines the emotional significance individuals with hoarding disorders attach to objects, suggesting that belongings may serve as sources of comfort or security, possibly stemming from deficiencies or traumatic experiences in childhood. Frost's studies explore the cognitive and behavioral patterns underlying hoarding, such as decision-making difficulties and a deep-seated need to save items, which could be influenced by early life traumas. While his research doesn't isolate childhood trauma as the whole contributing factor, it acknowledges that such experiences can significantly impact the development and intensity of hoarding behaviors.

PERFECTIONISM

Perfectionism is a personality trait characterized by a relentless pursuit of high standards, a strong desire for flawlessness, and an excessive concern over making mistakes or falling short of one's self-imposed expectations. Dr. Brene Brown, an esteemed researcher, has significantly contributed to the understanding of perfectionism, particularly highlighting its connection to childhood trauma. In her work, Brown portrays perfectionism as a coping mechanism, a shield used by individuals to protect themselves from criticism, judgment, and shame, driven by an underlying fear of inadequacy. She links this trait to experiences in childhood, such as exposure to trauma, criticism, or unrealistic expectations, where children adopt perfectionism as a means to secure approval and affirm their worthiness. This pursuit of flawlessness, as Brown elucidates, often undermines self-identity and leads to relentless self-criticism and emotional exhaustion. Central to her approach is the Shame-Resilience Theory, which advocates for acknowledging vulnerabilities and embracing imperfections as pathways to overcoming the negative impacts of perfectionism. Brown emphasizes the importance of authenticity and self-compassion, encouraging individuals to accept their true selves and imperfections as integral aspects of the human experience her work offers profound insights into the dynamics of perfectionism rooted in childhood experiences, providing guidance on fostering self-acceptance, resilience, a healthier sense of self-worth

OBSESSIVE COMPULSIVE DISORDER (OCD)

Obsessive Compulsive Disorder (OCD) is a complex mental health condition characterized by intrusive, distressing thoughts (obsessions) and repetitive behaviors or mental acts (compulsions). A study titled *The Impact of Childhood Trauma on the Onset and Course of Obsessive-Compulsive Disorder* published in the *Journal of Anxiety Disorders* by Wheaton et al. examined the relationship between childhood trauma and OCD. The study found that individuals with a history of childhood trauma, such as physical or sexual abuse, neglect, or other adverse childhood experiences, had a higher risk of developing OCD symptoms compared to those without such a history.

CHAPTER SUMMARY

- Lasting Effects of Trauma: Childhood trauma can have enduring psychological, physical, and emotional effects into adulthood.

- Mental Health Impact: Long-term consequences of trauma include depression, bipolar disorder, anxiety disorders, PTSD, and C-PTSD.

- Physical Health Correlations: Childhood trauma can lead to chronic pain and increased risk of cardiovascular and respiratory disorders.

- Behavioral Manifestations: Trauma may manifest as various behaviors in adulthood, including eating disorders and hoarding.

- Comprehensive Understanding and Healing: This chapter emphasizes the need for a holistic approach to understanding and healing from the long-term impacts of childhood trauma.

APPLY IT!

Journal Prompts

1. Depression/Bipolar and Childhood Trauma Connection: Reflect on your understanding of depression or bipolar disorder in the context of your childhood trauma. Write about how you see the connection between your past experiences and your current mental health.

2. Anxiety/PTSD and Trauma Impact: Consider your relationship with anxiety or PTSD. Journal about specific instances where you recognize the influence of your childhood trauma on these feelings.

3. Physical Health and Trauma Correlation: Think about any physical health issues you face, such as chronic pain or

cardiovascular problems. Write about how you believe these might be linked to your past traumatic experiences.

4. Coping Mechanisms Origin: Reflect on your coping mechanisms, such as hoarding or perfectionism. Write about how these behaviors may be tied to your childhood experiences and what they represent for you.

5. Identity Issues and Childhood Trauma: If you've struggled with identity issues, such as personality disorders, journal about how you think these struggles relate to your childhood experiences.

Suggested Goals

1. Mental Health Awareness Goal: Spend time each week learning about one of the conditions discussed in the chapter (e.g., depression, anxiety, PTSD) and how they relate to childhood trauma.

2. Coping Strategy Goal: Identify one unhelpful coping mechanism you currently use (like perfectionism or avoidance). Work on developing a healthier alternative over the next few months.

3. Support Network Goal: Aim to join a support group or therapy group specifically for survivors of childhood trauma, to share experiences and coping strategies.

4. Complete the exercises in Chapter 3 of the *Childhood Trauma and Recovery Workbook* to deepen your understanding and apply the concepts discussed.

4

Why Do I Feel Stuck in the Same Relationship Patterns?

NAVIGATING THE COMPLEX WEB OF ATTACHMENT AND INTERPERSONAL DYNAMICS

"We are born in relationship, we are wounded in relationship, and we can be healed in relationship." – Harville Hendrix

In the chapter titled "Social and Relationship Dynamics," we explore the profound impact of early childhood experiences on the formation of attachment styles and their subsequent influence on adult social interactions and relationships. This journey begins with a focus on the pivotal insights of Dr. Allan N. Schore, who emphasizes the critical role of the brain's right hemisphere in early emotional development. Dr. Schore's work illuminates how our earliest interactions and experiences, particularly those involving emotional attunement and response, shape the development of our capacity for emotional processing and regulation.

From there, we transition to examining the Secure Attachment Style, where early experiences of consistent and nurturing care lay the groundwork for healthy interpersonal relationships characterized by trust, open communication, and a balanced approach to intimacy and independence. We investigate the effects of Secure Attachment Disruption, where neglect of inconsistent caregiving in childhood leads to challenges in forming stable, trusting relationships in adulthood, often manifesting in social and emotional difficulties. The narrative further explores the Anxious-Preoccupied Attachment Style, emerging from a backdrop of unstable and unpredictable caregiving, leading to heightened sensitivity and a deep-seated need for closeness in adult relationships. Additionally, we address Dismissive-Avoidant Tendencies, where individuals, as a response to emotionally unavailable or dismissive early caregiving, adopt a stance of emotional self-reliance, often at the cost of deeper emotional connections. The last analysis of attachment style is of the Fearful-Avoidant (Disorganized) Attachment Style, a complex outcome of a trauma-filled chaotic childhood environment, which results in a conflicted approach to intimacy and trust in adult rela tionships.

In this chapter, we not only explore the different attachment styles and their childhood origins but also consider the social and relational consequences of these patterns. We explore how early traumatic experiences shape adult relationships and self-perception, often leading to challenges in trust, intimacy, and emotional regulation. The chapter concludes by addressing the significance of understanding and addressing these attachment styles, emphasizing the potential for healing and growth.

This exploration is an invitation to understand the intricate structure of our interpersonal relationships and the profound impact of our earliest life experiences. It's a journey that combines scientific insight with a compassionate understanding of human nature.

THE FOUNDATIONS OF ATTACHMENT: UNDERSTANDING STYLES AND CHILDHOOD ORIGINS

In this subchapter, we explore the roots of attachment theory, a cornerstone in understanding human relationships. Originating from the pioneering work of John Bowlby and Mary Ainsworth, attachment theory offers profound insights into how our earliest life experiences form the basis of our attachment styles, setting the foundation for how we connect with others throughout our lives. This exploration not only informs but also helps us understand the intricate patterns woven into the fabric of our interpersonal relationships.

SECURE ATTACHMENT STYLE

The key characteristics of a secure attachment style include:

- Comfort with intimacy and independence in relationships

- Trust in others and a positive view of relationships

- Open and honest communication with partners

- Effective emotional regulation and resilience in handling conflicts.

- Willingness to give and receive support in relationships.

- Confidence in one's worthiness of love and respect

These traits contribute to healthy, balanced, and fulfilling relationships. Individuals with a secure attachment style can generally form strong, lasting bonds based on mutual respect and understanding.

A secure attachment style typically develops in early childhood through consistent, responsive, and nurturing care from caregivers. When a child's emotional and physical needs are reliably met, they learn to trust their caregivers and feel safe exploring their environment. This consistent support fosters a sense of security and self-worth in the child, laying the foundation for healthy emotional development and the ability to form secure relationships in the future.

Secure attachment significantly influences emotional regulation and coping strategies. An individual with a secure attachment style generally has a strong foundation in managing their emotions effectively. They are better equipped to handle stress, process emotional experiences healthily, and recover from setbacks more resiliently. This stability in emotional regulation is often attributed to their early experiences of consistent care and support, which helps them develop a sense of security and trust in their relationships and themselves. As a result, they can approach life's challenges with confidence and a balanced perspective.

Secure attachment plays a crucial role in forming and maintaining healthy relationships. It fosters trust, open communication, and mutual respect, which are key ingredients for strong and lasting bonds. Securely attached individuals tend to approach relationships with a balanced view, able to express their needs and respond to their partner's needs effectively. This foundation of security and understanding supports healthy dynamics, conflict resolution, and emotional intimacy, leading to more fulfilling and resilient relationships.

Understanding secure attachment can be pivotal in the healing process from childhood trauma. It offers a framework for recognizing and aspiring towards healthier relationship patterns, distinct from those formed by traumatic experiences. This understanding can help in identifying maladaptive patterns and working towards cultivating traits of secure attachment, such as trust, effective emotional regulation, and open communication. It's a journey that involves self-awareness, learning from positive relationship models, and often therapeutic support, guiding individuals toward building more fulfilling and stable relationships.

SECURE ATTACHMENT DISRUPTION

Secure Attachment Disruption is a crucial aspect to consider, especially in the context of early childhood experiences and their long-term impact on an individual's mental health and relational patterns. A disruption in secure attachment, often due to neglect, abuse, or inconsistent caregiving in early life, can lead to a range of complex behavioral and emotional challenges.

In a case study reported by *BMC Psychiatry*, a young boy with a history of early life deprivation displayed various complex symptoms. Despite normal developmental assessments in certain areas, he exhibited significant behavioral and mood challenges, potentially related to disrupted attachment and a history of neglect. He also showed symptoms that might suggest underlying PTSD, Disinhibited Social Engagement Disorder (DSED), or even mood disorders. This case exemplifies the diagnostic complexity in children with disrupted attachment histories and the impacts of early life trauma on their development.

Furthermore, an article by the Momentous Institute highlights that children with disrupted attachments often exhibit behaviors that can be misinterpreted as troublesome or manipulative. These children might come across as self-sufficient or exceedingly charming, masking underlying feelings of insecurity and self-doubt. They often require a safe, predictable environment and consistent, supportive adult relationships to help them develop a sense of security and trust. This case exemplifies the diagnostic complexity in children with disrupted attachment histories and the impacts of early life trauma on their development.

Both these sources shed light on the complex nature of secure attachment disruption and the need for a nuanced, empathetic approach to caring for children with such experiences. They highlight the significant role of early childhood experiences in shaping mental health and the importance of early intervention and supportive relationships in mitigating the long-term effects of disrupted attachment.

THE ANXIOUS-PREOCCUPIED ATTACHMENT STYLE

The Anxious-Preoccupied Attachment Style is characterized by several key aspects, shaped by early childhood experiences and interactions with caregivers. Understanding these aspects is crucial in identifying and addressing this attachment style in both personal development and therapeutic settings:

- Heightened Need for Closeness and Approval: Individuals with this attachment style often exhibit an intense desire for closeness and approval from others. They may fear rejection or abandonment, leading to behaviors that seek constant reassurance and validation from their relationships.

- Sensitivity to Partners' Actions: They are highly sensitive to their partners' actions and moods, often interpreting even minor changes as signs of potential relationship problems. This sensitivity can lead to a tendency to overreact or misinterpret their partner's behaviors.

- Low Self-Esteem: Anxious-preoccupied individuals often struggle with self-esteem issues. They may rely heavily on their relationships for self-worth, feeling insecure or unworthy when they are not in a relationship or when their relationship is unstable.

- Difficulty with Trust and Dependency: Despite their desire for close relationships, they may have underlying trust issues, fearing that they will be let down or abandoned. This can result in a paradoxical pattern of craving intimacy while simultaneously struggling to fully trust and depend on their partner.

- Emotional Intensity and Volatility: Their relationships can be marked by emotional intensity and volatility. They might experience mood swings, intense emotional highs and lows, and strong reactions to perceived threats to the relationship.

- Clinginess and Overdependence: This attachment style often leads to clingy and overly dependent behaviors in relationships. Individuals might fear giving their partner space, worry excessively when apart, and struggle to maintain their independence within the relationship.

- Anxiety and Insecurity in Relationships: They often feel anxious about their relationship's stability and may doubt their partner's commitment, even in the absence of any real threat or issue.

- Overanalyzing and Ruminating: Anxious-preoccupied individuals may spend a significant amount of time analyzing their relationships, ruminating over interactions, and worrying about the status of their bonds.

- Impact on Relationship Dynamics: These characteristics can affect the dynamics of their relationships, sometimes leading to cycles of conflict and reconciliation, and challenges in establishing stable, mutually satisfying relationships.

An anxious-preoccupied attachment style is often formed in response to childhood trauma through a combination of inconsistent caregiving and the emotional unavailability of caregivers. This attachment style can develop in children who experience caregivers as unpredictably responsive. These caregivers may at times be nurturing, but at other times, they might be neglectful, overly intrusive, or emotionally unavailable.

Such inconsistency leaves the child in a state of confusion and anxiety about the availability and responsiveness of their caregivers. The child learns to constantly seek attention and validation, as their needs are only sometimes met. This pattern of attachment is characterized by heightened sensitivity to the caregiver's response and a deep-seated fear of abandonment or rejection.

This attachment style can also develop in children who witness or experience trauma such as domestic violence, substance abuse in the family, or severe illness. These experiences can disrupt the normal development of secure attachment, as the child's emotional needs are overshadowed by the chaotic or distressing environment.

Over time, these early experiences shape the child's expectations of relationships, leading to a heightened need for closeness and approval, fear of rejection, and difficulty trusting others in their adult relationships. The anxious-preoccupied attachment style reflects an adaptive response to an environment where care and affection are unpredictable, creating an ongoing struggle for security and connection.

DISMISSIVE-AVOIDANT TENDENCIES

Dissmissive-avoidant attachment, a style identified in attachment theory, is characterized by a tendency to maintain emotional distance in relationships. Individuals with this attachment style often prioritize independence and self-sufficiency over close emotional bonds Key aspects of dismissive-avoidant tendencies include:

- Emotional Distance: Individuals with a dismissive-avoidant attachment style are often emotionally distant and may struggle with intimacy and vulnerability in relationships. They might avoid or feel uncomfortable with too much closeness.

- High Value on Independence: They highly value their independence and self-reliance, often feeling that they don't need close relationships as much as others do. This can lead to a preference for solitary activities or hobbies.

- Difficulty Expressing Emotions: They often have trouble expressing their emotions and needs. This can manifest as a reluctance to share feelings or seek support during stressful times.

- Avoidance of Dependence: These individuals avoid situations where they might appear vulnerable or need to depend on others. They may withdraw from partners or friends during times of emotional need.

- Minimizing the Importance of Relationships: They tend to minimize or downplay the importance of relationships in their life, often focusing on work or hobbies instead.

- Skepticism about Love and Attachment: A dismissive-avoidant person may be skeptical about the value of close emotional bonds and may question the necessity of romantic relationships

- Self-Sufficiency as a Defense Mechanism: Their emphasis on self-sufficiency and independence is often a defense mechanism to protect against the perceived risks of being close or vulnerable to others

- Difficulty with Long-Term Relationships: They may have difficulty maintaining long-term relationships due to their tendency to pull away when things get too intimate or emotionally demanding.

- Perception of Self and Others: They often have a positive view of themselves but a more cautious, sometimes negative view of other people. They may believe that they are better off relying on themselves than trusting in others.

- Response to Conflict and Stress: In times of conflict or stress, they are more likely to withdraw or shut down emotionally, preferring to deal with issues on their own rather than seeking support or comforting the issue directly.

These tendencies can lead to challenges in forming and sustaining close, supportive relationships. For individuals with a dismissive-avoidant attachment style, recognizing and understanding these patterns can be the first step toward developing more secure attachment behaviors. Therapy and self-exploration can be effective in addressing these tendencies, helping to build stronger and more fulfilling relationships.

A dismissive-avoidant attachment style is often formed in response to childhood trauma through experiences where emotional needs were not adequately met. This style can develop when caregivers are emotionally unavailable or dismissive of the child's needs, leading to a sense of emotional self-sufficiency. The child learns to rely on themselves and often views close relationships as unnecessary or potentially disappointing. This coping mechanism, formed in response to the lack of consistent, nurturing care, manifests in adulthood as a preference for emotional distance and independence in relationships.

FEARFUL-AVOIDANT (DISORGANIZED) ATTACHMENT

Fearful-avoidant (Disorganized) Attachment, identified in attachment theory, is marked by ambivalence and inconsistency in relationships.

Individuals with this style often experience a mix of desire for and fear of intimacy, leading to complex relational dynamics. Key aspects of fearful-avoidant tendencies include:

- Conflicted Feelings About Intimacy: Desiring closeness but simultaneously fearing the vulnerability it entails.

- Trust Issues: Difficulty trusting others, often stemming from past relational traumas or betrayals.

- Emotional Turbulence: Experiencing intense, sometimes contradictory emotions in relationships.

- Fear of Abandonment and Rejection: Persistent worry about being abandoned or rejected, driving erratic behavior in relationships.

- Inconsistent Relational Behavior: Fluctuating between seeking closeness and pushing others away.

- Challenges in Emotional Regulation: Struggling with managing emotions, leading to unpredictable moods and responses.

- Relationship Instability: Tendency towards unstable and tumultuous relationships, marked by ongoing conflicts and unresolved issues.

Individuals with this attachment style often face difficulties in forming and maintaining stable, secure relationships.

Childhood trauma correlates with the development of a fearful-avoidant (disorganized) attachment style due to the unpredictable, unsafe, or chaotic environment experienced by the child. Trauma such as abuse, neglect, or witnessing violence disrupts the child's ability to form a stable attachment, leading to conflicting desires for closeness and fear of intimacy. This inconsistent caregiving environment creates confusion and fear, making it challenging for the child to develop secure attachment patterns. The resulting fearful-avoiding attachment style reflects these early traumatic experiences and their impact on the child's approach to relationships.

THE NEUROBIOLOGY OF ATTACHMENT

In the field of attachment theory and neurobiology, Dr. Allan N. Schore emphasizes the crucial role of the brain's right hemisphere during early human development. Known as the 'emotional brain,' this hemisphere is particularly active and influential in infancy, a time of rapid neural growth and development. Early in life, the right hemisphere begins developing, laying the foundation for emotional processing and stress management. This hemisphere is primarily responsible for processing and regulating emotions including interpreting emotional cues from caregivers. These interactions are critical for developing secure attachments and directly influence the development of the right hemisphere. Nonverbal communication, such as facial expressions, tone of voice, and body language, is vital in the attachment process during infancy. The right hemisphere plays a significant role in interpreting these cues, enabling infants to form emotional connections with their caregivers. It is also instrumental in forming emotional memories. The nature of these early memories – whether secure and comforting or anxious and fearful – shapes the child's emotional landscape and future stress responses. The development of the right hemisphere is pivotal in shaping the child's stress response system. A well-developed right hemisphere, nurtured through positive attachment experiences, can lead to a more balanced and effective stress response. Conversely, traumatic experiences can lead to an overactive or dysregulated stress response, increasing susceptibility to anxiety and mood disorders. The long-term implications of the right hemisphere's development in infancy are significant for emotional health. A strong and well-developed right hemisphere contributes to better emotional regulation, resilience, and social skills later in life.

Dr. Schore's focus on the right hemisphere highlights its essential role in early emotional development. The experiences and attachments formed in infancy have a direct impact on this hemisphere's development, setting the stage for an individual's emotional regulation capabilities, stress responses, and overall emotional health throughout life. This neurobiological perspective of attachment sheds light on the importance of nurturing and emotionally attuned caregiving in the earliest years of life. The concept of attachment and its role in emotional regulation is central to Dr. Schore's research. He emphasizes that the quality of early emotional interactions, especially between a child and their primary caregivers, is vital for the child's lifelong ability to regulate emotions. This development is closely linked to the growth and functioning of the brain's right hemisphere.

In early life, a child learns to regulate emotions primarily through interactions with caregivers, involving both verbal and nonverbal communication. These interactions are crucial in shaping the neural circuits responsible for emotional regulation. A caregiver's ability to attune to and appropriately respond to a child's emotional states is fundamental. This attunement, recognizing and responding to a child's needs and emotional cues, provides a model for the child to understand and manage their own emotions. During these formative years, the right hemisphere of the brain undergoes significant neural plasticity, allowing it to adapt and learn from emotional experiences. Positive, nurturing experiences strengthen the neural pathways that facilitate effective emotional regulation. Conversely, inconsistent, neglectful, or abusive caregiving can disrupt the development of these emotional regulation centers, leading to difficulties in emotion management, increased susceptibility to stress and anxiety, and challenges in forming healthy relationships later in life. Secure attachment, fostered by consistent and empathetic caregiving, enhances the child's ability to manage stress. The security and predictability provided by a responsive caregiver help develop a robust stress response system in the brain, particularly within the right hemisphere.

The patterns of emotional regulation established in early childhood have long-term implications. They affect how individuals manage their emotions internally and how they interact with others and form relationships. The ability to regulate emotions effectively is crucial for psychological well-being, resilience, and social competence. Dr. Schore's research highlights the interplay between attachment and emotional regulation, underscoring the crucial role of early caregiver-child interactions in the development of the right hemisphere and its capacity for emotional processing. These early experiences lay the foundation for a person's lifelong emotional landscape and stress management strategies, emphasizing the importance of nurturing and responsive caregiving in the early stages of life.

Emotional attunement, central to Dr. Schore's research on the neurobiology of attachment, is crucial for a caregiver's understanding and response to a child's emotional states. It is essential in developing secure attachment and significantly influences brain development, particularly in areas related to emotional and psychological health. Emotional attunement starts with the caregiver's ability to perceive and interpret a child's emotional cues, recognize signs of distress or happiness, and understand their meanings. Responsive interaction follows, where the caregiver meets the child's emotional needs with appropriate and timely responses. This consistency builds trust and security, helping the child learn that their emotions are valid and important.

Furthermore, through attuned interactions, children develop emotional regulation skills, internalizing their caregiver's responses as models for managing their feelings. This skill is vital for self-soothing and stress management. Emotional attunement also impacts neural development, particularly in the right hemisphere as mentioned before, which processes emotions. This stimulation aids in developing emotional intelligence, empathy, and social skills. The quality of emotional attunement in early life lays the groundwork for future relationships, with securely attached children more likely to form healthy, reciprocal, and emotionally fulfilling relationships as adults.

Additionally, emotional attunement and secure attachment offer resilience against psychological challenges, equipping children to better handle stress, adapt to change, and recover from setbacks. In conclusion, as Dr. Schore highlights, emotional attunement is vital in early development, not just for immediate emotional and psychological well-being but also for long-term emotional navigation and relationship building. Caregivers play a crucial role in this process, as their attuned responses directly influence the child's emotional development and brain maturation. Understanding and prioritizing emotional attunement are therefore critical in parenting, early childhood education, and therapeutic practices, particularly for children who have experienced trauma or attachment disruptions.

The consequences of maladaptive attachment, a key focus of Dr. Allan N. Schore's research, are significant and far-reaching. These negative outcomes arise when a child experiences neglect, abuse, or trauma, especially during crucial developmental periods, impacting the right brain's development. This can lead to profound difficulties in emotional regulation, heightened stress responses, and challenges in forming healthy relationships.

One primary consequence is impaired emotional regulation. The right hemisphere, crucial for processing and regulating emotions, may not develop optimally in cases of maladaptive attachment. This can result in difficulties in identifying, expressing, and managing emotions, leading to overwhelming emotions or emotional numbness. Traumatic early experiences can also lead to a dysregulated stress response system. The brain becomes overly sensitive to perceived threats, resulting in heightened and prolonged stress responses, even in non-threatening situations. This chronic hyperarousal can contribute to anxiety, depression, and other stress-related disorders.

Additionally, a history of abuse or neglect can create difficulties in forming secure attachments later in life. Individuals may struggle with trust, perceiving others as unreliable or potentially harmful, hindering the formation of close, healthy relationships. There are also social and emotional challenges. The right brain's ability to interpret social cues and emotions is compromised in cases of maladaptive attachment, leading to social misunderstandings, withdrawal, or conflict in relationships.

These attachment issues increase vulnerability to various mental health issues, such as mood disorders, personality disorders, and substance abuse, often used as coping mechanisms for unresolved trauma and emotional dysregulation. Moreover, chronic stress and emotional dysregulation can have direct impacts on physical health, contributing to cardiovascular problems, weakened immune response, and metabolic disorders.

Given these severe consequences, early intervention is crucial. Addressing maladaptive attachment issues early can mitigate adverse effects on brain development and emotional regulation. Interventions might include trauma-focused therapy, creating safe and nurturing environments, and providing consistent, empathetic caregiving.

In conclusion, the consequences of maladaptive attachment highlight the profound importance of early emotional experiences in shaping an individual's overall development. Understanding the impact of trauma, neglect, and abuse on the right brain's development and the subsequent challenges in emotional regulation and relationship formation is critical. This knowledge underscores the need for sensitive, informed approaches in therapeutic and caregiving contexts, especially for those who have experienced adverse early life experiences.

SOCIAL AND RELATIONAL CONSEQUENCES

This subchapter dives into the intricate ways childhood trauma shapes adult relationships and self-perception. We explore how experiences of mistrust, fear of betrayal, and challenges in finding deep connections often stem from early traumatic experiences. These issues profoundly affect one's ability to trust, share, and engage meaningfully with others. Additionally, we examine the profound impact of such trauma on self-identity, where struggles with self-concept, esteem, and decision-making reflect the lasting scars of early adversity. The chapter also addresses the fear of intimacy that many trauma survivors face, manifesting in a hesitancy to form close relationships due to associations of closeness with pain. Furthermore, we discuss the tendency towards social withdrawal, a protective but isolating response to past hurts, and the challenges in emotional regulation that exacerbate difficulties in handling life's stresses.

DIFFICULTY IN TRUSTING OTHERS

Individuals with difficulty in trusting others as a result of childhood trauma often experience a range of challenges in their interpersonal relationships. This difficulty can manifest in various aspects of their lives:

- Persistent Mistrust: A general suspicion or mistrust of others' intentions, often leading to reluctance in forming close relationships or friendships.

- Fear of Betrayal: Constant fear that others will betray or hurt them, as might have happened in their past

- Difficulty Opening Up: They might find it hard to share personal information or express emotions, fearing that this vulnerability could be exploited.

- Challenges in Relationships Building: Forming deep, meaningful relationships can be particularly challenging, as trust is a fundamental component of such connections.

- Interpreting Actions Negatively: There might be a tendency to misinterpret others' actions or words as negative or harmful, even when not intended that way.

Childhood trauma contributes to these trust issues by impacting the individuals' early experiences with caregivers or family members. Traumatic experiences, especially those involving betrayal, abuse, or neglect by trusted figures, can distort a person's perception of trust and safety. These experiences can lead the individual to develop a protective mechanism of mistrust to avoid further hurt or disappointment.

SELF-IDENTITY ISSUES

Childhood trauma can significantly impact the development of self-identity, as evidenced by various studies and research. One study focused on exploring the relationships between traumatic experiences and identity development, specifically among university students. It found that childhood traumas, particularly emotional abuse, were significantly associated with difficulties in emotional regulation and identity confusion. The prevalence of childhood traumas in the study group was notably high, and those from lower-income groups or with a history of self-harm or suicide attempts had significantly higher trauma scores. This study highlights the profound effects of childhood traumatic events on the development of a sense of identity and the potential association with self-harm behaviors in later stages of life.

Individuals with self-identity issues stemming from childhood trauma may experience a range of challenges and symptoms that affect their sense of self and overall well-being. Some of these experiences include:

- Poor Self Concept: Trauma can lead to a fragmented or distorted sense of self. Individuals might struggle with understanding who they are, leading to confusion about their values, beliefs, and goals.

- Low Self-Esteem: Childhood trauma often results in feelings of worthlessness or inadequacy. This can manifest as persistent self-doubt, negative self-talk, and a general lack of confidence.

- Difficulty Trusting Their Perceptions: Trauma can cause individuals to question their judgment and perceptions, leading to uncertainty in decision-making and self-doubt.

- Challenges in Forming and Maintaining Relationships: Self-identity issues can make it hard to establish and maintain healthy relationships. Individuals might struggle to understand their role in relationships or have difficulty expressing their needs and boundaries.

- Feeling Disconnected or Alienated: A sense of alienation from others is common, as individuals might feel that their experiences separate them from their peers or make them different in some fundamental way.

- Vulnerability to Mental Health Issues: Self-Ideitify issues can increase vulnerability to mental health problems like depression, anxiety, and personality disorders.

- Susceptibility to Re-victimization: A lack of strong self-identity can make individuals more vulnerable to further victimization or abusive relationships, as they may struggle to assert themselves or recognize unhealthy dynamics.

- Identify Confusion in Key Life Decisions: Trauma can make it challenging to make important life decisions, such as career choices, as individuals might lack a clear sense of what they want or what aligns with their authentic self.

In conclusion, the impacts of childhood trauma on self-identity are both profound and multifaceted. Research indicated a significant link between early traumatic experiences, particularly emotional abuse, and challenges in developing a stable sense of self. Individuals affected by such trauma often struggle with emotional regulation, self-esteem, and forming healthy relationships. These difficulties not only affect their sense of identity but also extend to various aspects of their lives, including mental health and decision-making.

FEAR OF INTIMACY

A person with a fear of intimacy as a result of childhood trauma might experience a range of emotional and relational challenges. This fear often stems from early experiences where trust was broken, such as in cases of neglect, abuse, or inconsistent caregiving. The individual learns to associate closeness with pain, leading to a protective mechanism of avoiding intimate relationships.

Key experiences and symptoms include:

- Reluctance to Form Close Relationships: They may avoid deep relationships or feel extremely anxious when relationships become more intimate

- Difficulty Trusting Others: Traumatic childhood experiences can lead to a deep-seated mistrust of others, making it hard for them to open up and trust someone fully.

- Emotional Distance: They might keep an emotional distance from others, even in seemingly close relationships, to protect themselves from potential hurt or betrayal.

- Challenges in Expressing Vulnerability: There can be significant difficulty in expressing vulnerabilities or sharing deep emotions with others.

- Overwhelming Anxiety in Close Situations: Intimate situations may trigger anxiety or fear, leading to withdrawal or avoidance behaviors

- Sabotaging Relationships: Subconsciously, they might sabotage relationships as they get closer to prevent perceived inevitable pain.

- Physical Discomfort from Affection: They may experience physical discomfort or anxiety with physical signs of affection.

Childhood trauma contributes to this fear by disrupting the normal development of trust and secure attachments in early life. The inconsistency or harmful nature of the relationships with primary caregivers creates a template for future relationships, where intimacy is equated with vulnerability and potential harm. This can result in a protective but maladaptive approach to relationships, viewing emotional closeness as threatening.

SOCIAL WITHDRAWAL OR ISOLATION

A person with social withdrawal or isolation as a result of childhood trauma may experience a range of emotional and behavioral responses that significantly impact their social interactions and relationships. The trauma endured in childhood, particularly in forms such as abuse, neglect, or witnessing violence, can profoundly affect their ability to connect with others and engage in social settings. Key experiences and symptoms can include:

- Avoidance of Social Situations: They may actively avoid social interactions and settings, finding them overwhelming or distressing.

- Feelings of Alienation: A sense of not belonging or feeling fundamentally different from others, often stemming from their traumatic experiences.

- Difficulty Trusting Others: Childhood trauma can lead to mistrust in others, making it challenging to form new relationships or engage in existing ones.

- Fear or Rejection or Judgment: They might fear being judged or rejected by others if they reveal their true selves or past experiences.

- Emotional Numbness or Detachment: A protective mechanism where the individual emotionally detaches from others to avoid potential hurt

- Increased Anxiety or Depression in Social Settings: Social interactions may trigger anxiety, panic, or depressive symptoms.

- Low Self-Esteem and Self-Worth: Feelings of worthlessness or inadequacy can lead to believing they don't deserve meaningful relationships.

Childhood trauma contributes to social withdrawal or isolation by impacting the individual's self-perception and their perception of others. Traumatic experiences, especially those involving primary caregivers, can disrupt the development of a healthy sense of self and a basic trust in others. This disruption can lead to viewing social relationships as potentially harmful or unfulfilling, prompting the individual to retreat and isolate themselves as a form of self-protection.

CHALLENGES IN EMOTIONAL REGULATION

Individuals who experience childhood trauma often face challenges in emotional regulation, which can manifest in various ways in their daily lives. The impact of trauma, especially when it occurs in critical developmental stages, can disrupt the natural development of emotional processing and regulation abilities. Here's what a person with such challenges might experience:

- Heightened Emotional Reactivity: Individuals might have intense emotional responses to situations that others may find manageable. This can include extreme sadness, anger, or fear in response to triggers that remind them of past trauma.

- Difficulty Identifying Emotions: They may struggle to recognize and name their emotions, which is essential for effectively managing them.

- Impulsive Responses: Trauma can lead to difficulty in controlling impulses, resulting in actions that are driven by emotions rather than rational thought.

- Mood Swings: Fluctuations in mood can be common, with rapid shifts from one emotional state to another.

- Dissociation: In some cases, individuals may dissociate or disconnect from their emotions as a coping mechanism, leading to periods of emotional numbness

- Overwhelm in Stressful Situations: They might find it challenging to cope with stress and may become quickly overwhelmed in situations that require emotional resilience

Childhood trauma contributes to these challenges by disrupting the brain's development related to emotional processing. Traumatic experiences can alter the way the brain responds to stress and emotions, leading to a heightened state of alertness or a shutdown response.

This can hinder the development of healthy coping mechanisms and emotional regulation strategies.

REPEATING PATTERNS OF ABUSE OR NEGLECT

Individuals who experience childhood trauma, especially in the form of abuse or neglect, may find themselves in a cycle of repeating these patterns in their adult lives. This repetition can manifest in various ways:

- Entering Abusive Relationships: They might unknowingly choose partners who replicate the abusive or neglectful dynamics they experienced in childhood. This is often due to a subconscious familiarity with such patterns.

- Perpetuating Abuse or Neglect: There is a risk of mirroring the behaviors learned in childhood when parenting their children or in other caregiving roles.

- Low Self-Esteem and Worthiness Issues: The trauma of abuse or neglect often leads to feelings of unworthiness, which can result in tolerating poor treatment from others.

- Difficulty Recognizing Unhealthy Patterns: Having grown up in an abusive or neglectful environment, they might not easily recognize these patterns as harmful, considering them normal or acceptable.

- Challenges in Establishing Boundaries: Trauma survivors often struggle with setting healthy boundaries, which can lead to repeated victimization or exploitation.

Childhood trauma contributes to these patterns by shaping one's understanding of relationships and self-worth. Traumatic experiences can become internalized, influencing beliefs about what they deserve or what relationships should look like This can lead to a subconscious gravitation towards situations that echo past traumas.

COMMUNICATION DIFFICULTIES

Individuals who have experienced childhood trauma might face significant challenges in communication, which can manifest in various aspects of their lives. These challenges are often a direct result of the coping mechanisms developed during their early traumatic experiences. Here's how these difficulties might present themselves:

- Struggle with Expression Emotions: Childhood trauma can lead to difficulties in identifying and expressing emotions. Individuals may struggle to articulate their feelings, leading to challenges in conveying their emotional state to others.

- Avoidance of Conflict: Due to fear of triggering negative reactions or reliving traumatic experiences, they might avoid confrontations or discussions about sensitive topics, even when necessary.

- Difficulty in Asserting Needs: Trauma survivors might find it hard to assert their needs or preferences in relationships or social settings, stemming from a fear of rejection or retaliation.

- Passive Communication Style: They may adopt a passive communication style, prioritizing others' needs and opinions over their own to avoid potential conflict or to gain approval.

- Withdrawal in Conversations: In response to triggers or discomfort, individuals might withdraw or shut down in conversations, finding it hard to stay engaged or responsive.

- Misinterpretation of Social Cues: Truma can impact the ability to accurately read and respond to social cues, leading to misunderstandings or inappropriate responses in social interactions.

Childhood trauma contributes to these communication difficulties by affecting the development of key social and emotional skills. Traumatic experiences, especially those involving caregivers, can disrupt the learning process of effective communication, emotional expression, and social interaction. For instance, if a child's emotional expressions are consistently ignored or punished, they may learn to suppress their emotions and avoid open communication as a survival mechanism.

IMPAIRED SOCIAL SKILLS

Individuals who have experienced childhood trauma often encounter difficulties in developing and utilizing social skills, as a consequence of their early adverse experiences. Here's how these challenges might manifest:

- Difficulty in Reading Social Cues: They might struggle to interpret facial expressions, body language, or vocal tones, which can lead to miscommunications or awkward social interactions.

- Challenges in Forming and Sustaining Friendships: Childhood trauma can make it difficult to form new friendships and maintain existing ones, often due to trust issues, fear or rejection, or a lack of understanding of social norms.

- Avoidance of Social Situations: Due to anxiety, fear, or past negative experiences, they may avoid social gatherings or interactions, leading to social isolation.

- Struggle with Verbal and Non-Verbal Communication: Trauma can impact both verbal and non-verbal communication skills, making it hard to engage effectively in conversations or to express oneself clearly.

- Overwhelm in Group Settings: large groups or unfamiliar social settings can be overwhelming, potentially triggering anxiety or stress.

- Reluctance to Share Personal Information: They might be overly guarded or reluctant to share personal details, stemming from a fear of being vulnerable.

Childhood trauma contributes to these social skill impairments by disrupting the natural developmental process where children learn and practice these skills. For example, if a child grows up in an environment where they are frequently criticized, ignored, or punished, they may not have the opportunity to develop healthy social interactions. Additionally, traumatic experiences can lead to hypervigilance or dissociation, which can further impede the development of social skills.

CHALLENGES IN PARENTING

Individuals who have experienced childhood trauma may face significant challenges in parenting, as the impact of their own traumatic experiences can influence their approach to raising children. Here are some ways these challenges might manifest:

- Difficulty in Emotional Regulation: Parents with a history of trauma may struggle with managing their emotions, which can affect their ability to respond calmly and consistently to their children's needs.

- Overptoectiveness or Neglect: They might become overly protective, stemming from their fears and anxieties, or conversely, they might lean towards neglect, replicating the patterns they experienced in childhood.

- Challenges in Establishing Boundaries: Struggling to set appropriate and consistent boundaries can stem from uncertainty about what constitutes healthy parenting.

- Repetition of Traumatic Patterns: There is a risk of unconsciously repeating abusive or neglectful behaviors experienced in their own childhood.

- Impaired Attachment with Children: Childhood trauma can affect a parent's ability to form secure attachments with their children, potentially leading to attachment issues in the next generation.

- Anxiety and Stress in Parenting: Parents may experience heightened anxiety and stress in their parenting role, especially in situations that remind them of their trauma.

Childhood trauma contributes to these challenges by influencing a person's emotional and psychological development. Traumatic experiences can alter perceptions of safety, trust, and relationships, which are central to effective parenting. For instance, a parent who experienced neglect might struggle to understand and meet their child's emotional needs adequately.

DIFFICULTY IN HANDLING CONFLICT

Individuals who have experienced childhood trauma often face difficulties in handling conflict in their adult lives. This challenge is rooted in the emotional and psychological impact of their early experiences. Here's how these difficulties might present:

- Avoidance of Conflict: They may avoid conflict altogether, fearing it could lead to violence, rejection, or abandonment, as might have been the case in their childhood experiences.

- Heightened Emotional Responses: Conflicts can trigger intense emotional reactions, such as anger or anxiety, making it hard for them to engage in calm and constructive discussions.

- Difficulty in Expressing Needs: Childhood trauma can lead to challenges in communicating one's needs and feelings effectively during conflicts, often due to fear of not being heard or respected.

- Fear of Escalation: there may be an underlying fear that any conflict, no matter how small, could escalate into something uncontrollable or dangerous.

- Struggle with Resolution: Finding and working towards a resolution can be challenging, as they might not have learned healthy conflict resolution skills in their formative years.

Childhood trauma contributes to these difficulties by impacting the development of key skills necessary for handling conflicts, such as emotional regulation, communication, and an understanding of healthy relational dynamics. For instance, if a child grows up in an environment where conflict is always met with aggression or avoidance, they may not learn how to engage in healthy, constructive conflict as adults.

SEEKING UNHEALTHY RELATIONSHIPS

Individuals who have experienced childhood trauma might often find themselves seeking or staying in unhealthy relationships in adulthood. This pattern can manifest in various ways and is deeply influenced by their early life experiences. here's how these tendencies might present:

- Attraction to Familiar Dynamics: They may be drawn to relationships that mirror the dynamics of their childhood, even if those are abusive or neglectful. This is often because such dynamics are familiar and, in a way, predictable.

- Low Self-Esteem: Childhood trauma can lead to low self-worth, which might make them feel undeserving of healthy, supportive relationships. As a result, they may tolerate poor treatment or abuse.

- Fear of Abandonment: If they experience abandonment or rejection in childhood, they might stay in unhealthy relationships due to a deep-seated fear of being alone or abandoned again.

- Difficulty Recognizing Red Flags: Their perception of what constitutes a normal or healthy relationship may be skewed due to their traumatic experiences, making it hard for them to recognize and respond to red flags.

- Repetition of Trauma: They might unconsciously recreate traumatic scenarios in an attempt to resolve unresolved issues from their past.

Childhood trauma contributes to these patterns by shaping one's beliefs about relationships and self-worth. Traumatic experiences, especially those involving primary caregivers, can establish a blueprint for future relationships where dysfunction or abuse is normalized. Additionally, trauma can impact one's ability to trust and connect with others, further complicating the pursuit of healthy relationships.

HYPER-VIGILANCE

Individuals with hyper-vigilance as a result of childhood trauma often experience heightened states of alertness and sensitivity to their surroundings. This condition can manifest in several ways:

- Constant Alertness: A continuous state of being on guard, anticipating danger or threat, even in safe environments.

- Heightened sensitivity to Environmental Cues: They may react intensely to sounds, movements, or other stimuli that others might not notice or consider harmful.

- Difficulty Relaxing: A persistent sense of anxiety can make it hard to relax or feel at ease, often leading to problems with sleep and concentration

- Overatction to Triggers: Situations that remind them of past trauma, even remotely, can trigger disproportionate emotional and physical responses.

- Social Anxiety: Fear and suspicion in social situations, leading to challenges in forming and maintaining relationships.

Childhood trauma contributes to hyper-vigilance by programming the brain to perpetually anticipate and respond to threats. Traumatic experiences, especially those involving physical or emotional danger, can lead to a heightened stress response system. This heightened state was once a necessary survival mechanism in an unpredictable or dangerous environment but becomes maladaptive when the threat is no longer present.

Chapter Summary

- Early traumatic experiences shape one's attachment style in adulthood. Secure attachments may become challenging to form, while anxious or avoidant behaviors in relationships are often rooted in unresolved childhood trauma.

- Trauma in childhood can lead to difficulties in establishing trust and achieving intimacy in adult relationships. The fear of vulnerability and the expectation of betrayal are common challenges.

- Childhood trauma survivors might develop coping mechanisms that influence their adult relationships. This could include patterns of codependency, emotional withdrawal, or repeating cycles of conflict and reconciliation.

- Acknowledging unhealthy relationship patterns, often a legacy of childhood trauma, is the first step towards healthier interactions.

- Therapeutic intervention and self-awareness can lead to healthier relationships. Healing from childhood trauma develops new, positive relationship patterns and fosters growth and understanding.

Apply It!

Journal Prompts

1. Understanding Attachment Style: Reflect on your own attachment style and how it may have been influenced by your childhood experiences. Consider how this style affects your current relationship.

2. Past Trauma's Impact on Relationship Responses: Write about a time when your response in a relationship was influenced more by past trauma than the present situation. How did this

awareness help you understand your reactions better?

3. Emotional Attunement in Relationships: Consider the concept of emotional attunement discussed by Dr. Allan N. Schore. Journal about how this resonates with your experiences of emotional connection or disconnection in relationships.

4. Desired Changes: What aspects of your attachment style would you like to change or improve? How do these desired changes align with your current understanding of healthy relationships?

5. Trust Issues and Childhood Influence: Write about your experiences with trust in relationships. How has your childhood impacted your ability to trust, and what steps could you take to build healthier trust patterns?

6. Learning from Past Relationships: Reflect on a past relationship and analyze how your attachment style played a role in its dynamics. What lessons can you draw from this reflection for future relationships?

Suggested Goals

1. Complete a validated attachment style questionnaire to understand your attachment style better. Reflect on the results and write down how this style might be influencing your current relationships.

2. For the next month, make a daily log of behaviors in your relationships that reflect your attachment style. Aim to identify one behavior per day and note it down, along with the context in which it occurred.

3. Choose a book by a renowned author on attachment theory (like John Bowlby or Mary Ainsworth) and read it over the next two months.

4. Complete the exercises in Chapter 4 of the *Childhood Trauma and Recovery Workbook* to deepen your understanding and apply the concepts discussed.

5

Why Do My Past Traumas Still Affect Me?

Understanding Triggers

"Until you make the unconscious conscious, it will direct your life and you will call it fate." – Carl Jung

What Exactly are Triggers

In entering the recovery stage of childhood trauma, understanding what triggers are and how they function is essential. Triggers are stimuli that evoke powerful emotional and physiological responses, deeply connected to past traumatic experiences. This subchapter aims to unpack the various dimensions of triggers, highlighting their intricate relationship with the brain's processing of trauma, the role of implicit memory, the implications of the Polyvagal Theory, and the nuanced impact of microtriggers and digital media.

Through this exploration, we aim to provide a deeper understanding of triggers, enhancing the knowledge necessary for effective coping and recovery strategies in the journey of healing from childhood trauma.

Sensory Triggers and The Brain

The Brain's Response to Sensory Information

Sensory triggers are deeply intertwined with the brain's processing of traumatic experiences, particularly in the context of childhood trauma. The brain's limbic system, specifically the amygdala, plays a crucial role in this process. When a person encounters sensory inputs (such as sounds, smells, or sights) that are reminiscent of those experienced during a traumatic event, the amygdala, which is key in emotional processing, can trigger a reactivation of the traumatic response. This phenomenon is often automatic and can occur outside of conscious awareness.

Neural Pathways and Trauma Recall

The neural pathways formed during traumatic events are robust and long-lasting. Sensory experiences associated with trauma can become deeply ingrained in these neural pathways. When similar sensory experiences occur later in life, they can prompt these pathways to reactivate, often leading to a vivid re-experience of the original emotional state associated with the trauma. This reaction is not just a recalled memory; it's an emotional and physiological state being re-lived.

Sensory Processing and Trauma

Research has shown that individuals with a history of childhood trauma may process sensory information differently. A study in the *Journal of Traumatic Stress* highlighted that certain sounds, smells, or visual cues could evoke intense emotional reactions in individuals with traumatic backgrounds. These sensory triggers are highly individualized, with each person having specific triggers based on their unique experiences.

The Role of the Hippocampus

In addition to the amygdala, the hippocampus – a region of the brain associated with memory formation and storage – is also involved in processing traumatic events. While the amygdala reacts to the emotional content of the trauma, the hippocampus is involved in contextualizing the event. However, under high stress, the functioning of the hippocampus can be impaired, leading to fragmented or disorganized memories associated with sensory triggers.

COMMON SENSORY TRIGGERS

Sensory triggers vary widely among individuals with childhood trauma, often linked to specific experiences. Common triggers include loud noises, particular voices or music, visual scenes or objects reminiscent of the trauma, familiar scents, physical sensations or contacts, and specific flavors. These triggers involuntarily evoke powerful emotional and physical responses related to past trauma, and recognizing them is a crucial step in recovery.

IMPLICIT MEMORY AND TRIGGERS

THE NATURE OF IMPLICIT MEMORY

Implicit memory, a concept explored extensively in the field of psychology, refers to memories that affect behavior and emotions without conscious awareness. This type of memory is particularly relevant in the context of childhood trauma, as traumatic experiences often become deeply ingrained in an individual's implicit memory system. Unlike explicit memories, which are conscious and can be recalled deliberately, implicit memories are automatic and can influence reactions and feelings without the person being aware of their origin.

HOW IMPLICIT MEMORY WORKS WITH TRAUMA

In childhood trauma, experiences are encoded not just as explicit memories but also as implicit memories. These implicit memories can include sensory experiences, emotional states, and physical reactions that were present during the traumatic event. Because they are not consciously recalled, these memories can be more challenging to identify and address.

According to a study published in the *Journal of Traumatic Stress*, the implicit memory of trauma can be triggered by experiences that are reminiscent of the original traumatic event, even if they are not consciously recognized as such. This can result in a traumatic response, such as anxiety, fear, or a physical reaction, seemingly without any apparent reason.

THE ROLE OF THE BRAIN IN IMPLICIT MEMORY

Neuroscientific research has shed light on how the brain processes and stores implicit memories. Key brain areas involved include the amygdala, which processes emotional reactions, and the hippocampus, which is crucial for forming explicit memories. In the case of trauma, the amygdala's response can be powerful and immediate, bypassing the more rational processing of the hippocampus. This often leads to the automatic, emotion-driven responses characteristic of triggered implicit memories.

CASE STUDIES

Case studies in clinical psychology provide insights into how implicit memory functions in survivors of childhood trauma. For instance, a case study detailed in Trauma, Violence, & Abuse highlighted an individual who experienced panic attacks in crowded spaces without understanding why. Through therapy, it was revealed that these spaces triggered implicit memories of childhood abuse, explaining the panic attacks.

EXAMPLES OF IMPLICIT MEMORY

Implicit memory in the context of childhood trauma can manifest in various ways, often as automatic responses or feelings that are triggered without the individual's conscious awareness. Here are some examples:

1. Physical Reactions: An individual might experience a sudden increase in heart rate, sweating, or a feeling of panic in certain situations without understanding why. For instance, being in a small, enclosed space might trigger a physical response due to a past traumatic event that occurred in a similar setting.

2. Emotional Responses: Feelings of fear, anger, sadness, or discomfort can arise in specific contexts, seemingly without reason. For example, a person might feel inexplicably anxious or fearful in the presence of someone who resembles a figure from their past trauma, even if they don't consciously recognize the resemblance.

3. Sensory Sensitivities: Certain sounds, smells, or textures might elicit a strong emotional or physical response. Someone might become distressed by the smell of a particular cologne or the

sound of a certain type of voice, not realizing these are linked to traumatic memories.

4. Behavioral Patterns: Unconscious coping mechanisms or avoidance behaviors can develop as a result of implicit memories. A person might habitually avoid certain discussions, places, or people without fully understanding their aversion, due to these elements being connected to past trauma.

5. Interpersonal Dynamics: Implicit memories can influence how an individual reacts in relationships or social interactions. They might find themselves feeling disproportionately mistrustful, defensive, or submissive around certain people, mirroring dynamics from traumatic childhood experiences.

6. Physical Discomfort or Symptoms: Unexplained physical symptoms like headaches, stomach aches, or muscle tension can occur in situations that subconsciously remind the person of their trauma. This is the body's way of responding to an implicit memory trigger.

7. Dreams and Nightmares: Traumatic memories can resurface in dreams or nightmares, often in a symbolic or non-literal form. These dreams might not directly replay the traumatic event but could evoke the same emotions or themes.

8. Automatic Skills or Knowledge: Skills or knowledge acquired during traumatic periods might be retained and performed automatically For example, a person might have learned to navigate their environment very quietly to avoid attracting negative attention and continue to move quietly as an adult.

These examples illustrate how implicit memories formed during childhood trauma can persist and manifest in daily life, influencing a person's reactions and behaviors without their explicit understanding. Recognizing and addressing these implicit memories is often a significant part of the healing process in trauma therapy.

THE POLYVAGAL THEORY AND TRIGGERS

INTRODUCTION TO POLYVAGAL THEORY

The Polyvagal Theory, developed by Dr. Stephen Porges, offers a groundbreaking perspective on how the autonomic nervous system responds to stress and trauma, particularly relevant to childhood trauma. This theory emphasizes the role of the vagus nerve, which regulates heart rate and respiratory rate, in controlling our responses to safe and threatening environments.

THE THREE-PART MODEL

According to Polyvagal Theory, there are three distinct subsystems within the vagus nerve, each linked to a different behavioral response:

1. The Ventral Vagal Complex: Associated with social engagement and feeling safe. It's active when we feel calm and connected.

2. The Sympathetic Nervous System: Triggers the 'fight or flight' response during perceived danger.

3. The Dorsal Vagal Complex: Engages in response to overwhelming stress, leading to a 'freeze' or shutdown state.

TRIGGERS AND THE POLYVAGAL THEORY IN CHILDHOOD TRAUMA

In the context of childhood trauma, triggers can involuntarily activate these autonomic responses. For example, a traumatic trigger could cause someone to involuntarily enter a 'fight, flight, or freeze' state. A study in the *Journal of Traumatic Stress* demonstrates how individuals with a history of trauma may have a heightened sympathetic response to certain triggers, leading to rapid heart rate, anxiety, or panic.

VENTRAL VAGAL ACTIVATION IN SAFE ENVIRONMENTS:

A child abuse survivor might experience a sense of calm and safety in a supportive environment, leading to ventral vagal activation. This could be observed in therapy, where a trusting relationship with the therapist helps them feel secure, reducing trauma-related responses.

SYMPATHETIC NERVOUS SYSTEM ACTIVATION BY TRIGGERS:

- Fight Response: An individual who was frequently criticized as a child might react with anger or defensiveness when receiving constructive feedback, a sympathetic 'fight' response triggered by past trauma.

- Flight Response: A person who experienced abandonment might feel an overwhelming urge to leave or disengage from intimate settings, a sympathetic 'flight' response to situations that subconsciously remind them of past trauma.

DORSAL VAGAL SHUTDOWN IN OVERWHELMING SITUATIONS:

- Freeze Response: In situations that feel uncontrollable or overwhelming, a trauma survivor might 'freeze' or dissociate. For instance, being in a crowded, noisy environment might trigger a shutdown response, mirroring the helplessness felt during childhood trauma.

- Fawning Response: A less discussed aspect is the 'fawn' response, where an individual might become excessively accommodating or submissive in response to certain triggers, a survival strategy developed during traumatic childhood experiences.

MIX OF RESPONSES IN COMPLEX TRIGGERS:

Some triggers might evoke a mix of responses. For example, a survivor of childhood neglect might initially engage in 'flight' behavior (like withdrawing) when feeling ignored but then switch to a 'freeze' state (like feeling numb) if withdrawal doesn't alleviate their distress.

CASE STUDY ILLUSTRATIONS

In a case study published in a trauma-focused journal, a patient with a history of childhood trauma showed a pattern of 'freezing' during conflict. Therapy sessions revealed that conflicts triggered a dorsal vagal response, a pattern traceable to childhood experiences of domestic violence where freezing was a coping mechanism.

Understanding these examples within the framework of the Polyvagal Theory can provide a deeper insight into the complex dynamics of trauma triggers and the body's automatic responses. This understanding is key to developing more effective therapeutic strategies for those recovering from childhood trauma.

MICROTRIGGERS AND CUMULATIVE EFFECTS

UNDERSTANDING MICROTRIGGERS

Microtriggers are small, often subtle triggers that, on their own, might not cause a significant emotional or physical response but can have a cumulative, stressful impact over time. These triggers are particularly relevant in the context of childhood trauma, where repeated exposure to certain stimuli or environments can lead to a buildup of stress and trauma responses.

CHARACTERISTICS OF MICROTRIGGERS

Microtriggers can be everyday occurrences or environmental factors that are usually overlooked but can gradually evoke a trauma response. These could include certain words, tones of voice, gestures, environmental cues, or even specific times of the day. Unlike more obvious triggers, microtriggers can be challenging to identify due to their subtlety and ubiquity.

CUMULATIVE EFFECTS OF MICROTRIGGERS

The cumulative effect of microtriggers is a critical concept in understanding childhood trauma. Each microtrigger may slightly activate the body's stress response, and over time, these small activations can accumulate, leading to heightened anxiety, stress, or a sense of being constantly 'on edge'. This concept aligns with research in the *Journal of Traumatic Stress*, which suggests that ongoing, low-level stressors can exacerbate symptoms of PTSD and other trauma-related disorders.

THE ROLE OF SENSITIZATION

Sensitization is a process where, after repeated exposure to stressors (including microtriggers), an individual becomes more reactive to these stimuli. This heightened reactivity can make everyday situations feel increasingly stressful or overwhelming. Sensitization is often discussed in trauma-focused literature, illustrating how trauma survivors can develop an amplified response to seemingly minor triggers over time.

Microtriggers and their cumulative effects offer a nuanced understanding of how ongoing, subtle stressors can significantly impact individuals with a history of childhood trauma. Recognizing and addressing these microtriggers is key to reducing their impact and supporting long-term recovery and resilience.

DIGITAL AND SOCIAL MEDIA TRIGGERS

THE DIGITAL LANDSCAPE AND CHILDHOOD TRAUMA

In the modern digital age, social media and online platforms have become integral to daily life. However, for individuals with a history of childhood trauma, these digital spaces can also become sources of triggers. Digital and social media triggers refer to content, interactions, or experiences online that can evoke trauma responses.

TYPES OF DIGITAL TRIGGERS

1. Visual Content: Images or videos that resemble or recall aspects of the traumatic experience can act as powerful triggers. This could include scenes of violence, depictions of abuse, or even specific places or objects related to the trauma.

2. Textual Content: Reading stories, comments, or posts that detail traumatic experiences similar to the individual's own can trigger emotional responses. Even seemingly innocuous words or phrases might be triggering if they are associated with past trauma.

3. Interpersonal Dynamics: Online interactions can mirror harmful dynamics from the individual's past, such as cyberbullying mirroring childhood bullying, or certain communication patterns echoing past abusive relationships.

IMPACT OF DIGITAL TRIGGERS

Digital triggers can lead to a range of responses, including anxiety, panic attacks, flashbacks, or emotional dysregulation. The pervasive nature of digital media means that individuals can encounter these triggers unexpectedly and frequently, which can exacerbate symptoms of PTSD or other trauma-related conditions.

HOW CAN I IDENTIFY MY PERSONAL TRIGGERS?

Identifying personal triggers is an essential step for individuals healing from childhood trauma, primarily because it fosters enhanced self-awareness and prevention of re-traumatization. Understanding one's triggers allows for a deeper insight into how past experiences continue to influence present reactions and behaviors, paving the way for more effective emotional regulation. This awareness is critical not only for individual well-being but also for improving interpersonal relationships, as it enables clearer communication of needs and boundaries. Additionally, recognizing triggers is vital in therapeutic settings, allowing for tailored interventions that specifically address these sensitives Therapies such as Cognitive Behavioral Therapy (CBT) and Eye Movement Desnsitiation and Reprocessing (EMDR) can be more effectively focused when triggers are clearly identified. Moreover, knowing one's triggers empowers individuals, granting them a greater sense of control over their trauma responses and reducing reliance on avoidance behaviors. This empowerment is a significant step towards promoting mindfulness, enabling individuals to distinguish between past trauma and present reality. Ultimately, the process of identifying and managing triggers is integral to the healing journey, contributing to overall mental and emotional well-being and fostering resilience.

Maintaining a journal to note emotional and physical discomforts, along with environmental and sensory details, helps in recognizing trigger patterns. Consulting with a therapist can deepen an understanding of past experiences affecting current reactions.

Primary Indicators:

1. Emotional Responses: Intense, sudden emotions like fear, anger, sadness, or panic disproportionate to the situation

2. Physical Sensations: Changes in the body such as a rapid heartbeat, sweating, trembling, or feeling frozen.

3. Flashbacks or Intrusive Thoughts: Vivid, involuntary memories of the trauma or persistent negative thoughts.

4. Behavioral Changes: Avoidance behaviors, heightened irritability, or a strong urge to escape.

5. Disassociation: A sense of detachment from reality or self, feeling like an observer of one's own experiences.

6. Cognitive Disruptions: Difficulty concentrating, confusion, or memory lapses directly related to the trauma.

SUBTLE INDICATORS:

1. Mood Fluctuations: Subtle mood changes in response to certain environments of conversations.

2. Physical Discomfort: Mild physical symptoms like stomachaches or headaches in specific situations.

3. Minor Avoidance: Avoiding certain topics of conversation or mildly changing behvaior in specific settings.

4. Low-Level Anxiety: persistent but low-level anxiety in certain situations that remind you of past trauma.

WHY DO CERTAIN SEEMINGLY NORMAL SITUATIONS OR WORDS GET TO ME?

Trauma significantly impacts how memories are stored and retrieved in the brain. During traumatic events, the brain forms strong associations between the sensory inputs present at the time (such as sights, sounds, or words) and the traumatic experience itself. As a result, even ordinary stimuli that resemble these inputs can later trigger a recall of the trauma. This recall is not just a simple memory but often comes with intense emotional and physical reactions, as the brain reacts as if the traumatic event is occurring again. This process highlights the deep and complex nature of how trauma affects memory and perception. From a psychological perspective, these reactions are part of the brain's defense mechanism. The brain, particularly the amygdala, becomes hyper-vigilant in recognizing patterns similar to those experienced during trauma. This vigilance, while initially a survival strategy, can become overactive, causing strong reactions to normal stimuli.

For individuals with PTSD, often rooted in childhood trauma, reactions to normal situations or words can be intense due to the brain's unique processing of traumatic memories. A Yale University study shows that when recalling trauma, brain activity in PTSD sufferers is significantly different and more fragmented, especially in the hippocampus. This leads to difficulty in recalling traumatic events coherently and makes ordinary stimuli trigger intense responses. Trauma alters memory storage and retrieval, associating everyday sensory inputs with the trauma, causing these stimuli to later trigger traumatic recall, accompanied by strong emotional and physical reactions. These insights highlight the complex impact of trauma on memory and perception and the need for specialized therapy to help integrate these fragmented memories.

How Do I Differentiate Between a Real Threat and a Triggered Response?

A real threat refers to an immediate and present danger, a situation where a person's safety is actually at risk. It triggers a response from the body's natural fight-or-flight mechanism, which is designed to protect us from harm. On the other hand, a triggered response, particularly in the context of PTSD or past trauma, is an emotional or physical reaction to a stimulus that resembles or reminds one of a past traumatic event. This reaction is often disproportional to the actual situation and is rooted in the trauma rather than a present threat. Understanding and distinguishing between these two types of responses is critical for individuals dealing with PTSD or trauma-related symptoms.

The challenge of differentiating between a real threat and a triggered response in individuals with PTSD, often rooted in childhood trauma, has been the subject of various studies. One significant aspect of this research is the understanding of how the brain processes and reacts to these stimuli.

In PTSD, the brain's response to trauma-related triggers is often exaggerated and different from its response to actual threats. Studies, including one that examined fear-potentiated startle in PTSD patients, have shown that the brain's fear response to trauma-related cues is more intense compared to the response to general threats or non-trauma-related stimuli. Another study involving functional MRI scans demonstrated an exaggerated amygdala response in PTSD patients when they were exposed to masked facial stimuli. The amygdala, a critical region in the brain for emotion processing, particularly fear, tends to be hyperactive in PTSD patients, leading to heightened responses to trauma-related cues.

Moreover, research on the hippocampus, the brain's memory-forming area, reveals distinct patterns when PTSD patients recall traumatic experiences compared to when they recall sad or neutral memories. This difference suggests that the brain processes traumatic memories in a fragmented and disorganized manner, which can contribute to the difficulty in differentiating between actual threats and triggered responses.

In understanding PTSD, it's also important to consider how Rapid Eye Movement (REM) sleep, a critical stage of sleep associated with dreaming and memory processing, interacts with PTSD symptoms. Disrupted REM sleep impairs the brain's ability to process and integrate traumatic memories appropriately. This impairment can lead to heightened, inappropriate responses to trauma-related cues, as the brain struggles to distinguish past trauma from current, actual threats. Proper REM sleep is essential for emotional regulation and memory consolidation; its disruption in PTSD patients thus exacerbates their difficulty in differentiating between real and perceived threats.

These studies collectively indicate that PTSD triggers can elicit responses in the brain that are distinct from those elicited by real threats. This knowledge is crucial for developing more effective therapeutic strategies to help individuals with PTSD distinguish between actual danger and triggers related to past trauma.

COMMON TRIGGERS

Triggers can vary widely from person to person, but here are some common examples:

1. Loud Noises or Yelling: Sudden loud sounds or someone raising their voice can trigger anxiety or fear, especially if the person experienced trauma in a volatile environment

   - Examples: Suden Loud Bangs, like fireworks or car horns, people raising their voices during an argument, or loud public spaces, such as concerts or sports events.

2. Specific Phrases or Words: Certain words or phrases that were used during the traumatic period, even if they are common or benign in other contexts, might trigger a strong emotional reaction.

   - Examples: "You're just like your father/mother.", "Stop being so dramatic.", or "You always/never do this.".

3. Unexpected Physical Contact: A sudden touch, even if friendly or consoling, can be startling and uncomfortable, particularly for those who have experienced physical or sexual abuse.

   - Examples: Someone tapping your shoulder to get your attention, a hug from a person you're not close with, or accidental bumping in crowded places

4. Seeing Similar Family Dynamics: Observing family interactions that mirror the dysfunctional or abusive dynamics from their childhood can trigger distress or anxiety.

   - Examples: Observing a parent scolding their child in public, a TV show portraying an overbearing parent, or hearing a friend talk about their strict family rules.

5. Authority Figures: Interacting with people in positions of authority, like bosses or officials, might trigger feelings of powerlessness or fear, especially if the trauma involves authority figures.

   - Examples: Being called into your boss's office unexpectedly, police officers stopping you for a routine check, or interactions with high-raking professionals in formal settings.

6. Crowded Places: Being in a crowded or chaotic environment can be overwhelming and trigger feelings of panic or loss of control.

   - Examples: Shopping malls during peak hours, packed public transportation, or crowded elevators

7. Feeling Trapped or Constrained: Situations where the person feels they cannot easily leave, such as being in a crowded room or a meeting, can evoke feelings of helplessness or panic.

   - Examples: Stuck in traffic with no alternative routes, long meetings or events with no clear end time, or situations where you're expected to stay, like a religious service or family dinner.

8. Conflict, Even if Minor: Experiencing or witnessing conflict, even if it's minor and non-violent, can be triggering for someone with a trauma history, especially if they grew up in an environment where conflict was frequent and intense.

   - Examples: Colleagues debating heatedly over a project, spouses or partners bickering over household decisions, or children arguing or fighting.

WHAT ARE SOME UNCOMMON TRIGGERS?

We often go through life not realizing that we are triggered. Some triggers that may be less obvious include:

- Feedback: Positive feedback can trigger shame, as it may feel manipulative or insincere, not aligning with the survivor's self-perception. Negative feedback can be devastating, especially if criticism in childhood is harsh and unfair. Neutral feedback is particularly troubling due to its ambiguity, leading to rumination and distrust.

- Ambiguity: Situations lacking clarity, like waiting for news or uncertain outcomes, can be deeply unsettling. This stems from a need for external validation of safety and security, a result of unstable or unpredictable environments in childhood.

- Other People's Moods: Hypervigilance regarding others' moods is common, with a tendency to feel responsible for or preoccupied with what others might be feeling, a behavior developed from having to constantly adjust to the moods of toxic or inconsistent caregivers in childhood.

- Being Misunderstood or Facing Anger: Experiencing misunderstanding or someone else's anger can lead to intense rumination and a desire to clarify or defend oneself. This often comes from childhood experiences of being unfairly judged or misunderstood by caregivers.

- Saying No and Mind Reading: Difficulty in saying no and expecting others to anticipate one's needs without communication is a common trigger. This arises from childhood experiences where expressing needs was shamed, leading to resentment and a tendency to over-commit.

- Thoughtless and Oblivious People Encountering people who seem self-absorbed or inconsiderate can trigger intense reactions, often linked to childhood experiences with self-consumed, oblivious caregivers. This leads to moral policing and internal conflict about others' behaviors.

STRATEGIES FOR MANAGING TRIGGERS

Navigating through triggers, especially those rooted in childhood trauma, can be challenging. This subchapter provides practical, detailed strategies to manage such triggers effectively.

1. Identify and Understand Your Triggers

- Awareness: Start by recognizing the physical and emotional sensations when triggered, as previously discussed, such as a rush of anger or a feeling of shutting down.

- Narrative Clues: Pay attention to the thoughts that accompany these sensations. For example, if a colleague's comment makes you feel undervalued, it might trigger a narrative of not being heard, echoing childhood experiences.

2. Acknowledge the Brain's Response (Emotional Brain vs. Rational Brain)

- Limbic Activation: In moments of being triggered, the limbic system, particularly the amygdala, becomes hyperactive. This part of the brain is responsible for processing emotions, memories, and survival instincts. It reacts instantaneously to perceived threats, often based on past traumas or intense experiences. This reaction is a protective mechanism, but in the context of non-threatening triggers, it can lead to disproportionate emotional responses.

- Prefrontal Cortex Shutdown: As the limbic system flares up, it effectively dampens the functioning of the prefrontal cortex. This part of the brain is crucial for thinking clearly, making balanced decisions, and regulating emotions. When it's offline, you're less able to think rationally, communicate effectively, or consider the long-term consequences of your actions.

- Example: When your partner comes home in a bad mood, it may trigger an immediate reaction of unease or anxiety, a response deeply rooted in the limbic system of your brain. This reaction often ties back to childhood experiences, such as dealing with an unpredictable parent, leading your brain to brace for negative outcomes in similar situations. Recognizing this pattern is crucial; it's not just the current mood affecting you but a learned response from your past. By acknowledging this, you can engage your prefrontal cortex to rationalize the situation, reminding yourself that the current scenario is different from your past. This understanding enables you to respond more calmly and rationally, such as giving your partner space or discussing the matter when you're both more composed, thus differentiating past traumas from present realities.

3. Anticipate Your Response to Being Triggered

○ Predictive Awareness: Once you realize you're triggered, anticipate how you typically react in such situations.

○ Example: If a joke you made in a meeting falls flat and you feel embarrassed, triggering a sense of failure, predict your usual response pattern. Perhaps you tend to withdraw or overcompensate with more jokes. Recognizing this pattern allows you to choose a different, more constructive response.

○ Humor as a Tool: If appropriate, use humor to acknowledge your overreaction internally. For example, think to yourself, "There I go again, making a mountain out of a molehill." This self-awareness, coupled with a light-hearted approach, can help defuse the intensity of the trigger.

4. Mindful Reaction vs. Overreaction

○ Implementing a Pause: When a trigger occurs and you feel the urge to react impulsively, consciously implement a brief pause. This could mean taking deep breaths, stepping away from the situation, or simply closing your eyes for a moment. The aim is to create a buffer between the trigger and your response.

○ Example in Practice: Imagine you receive an email from your boss that criticizes your recent work. Your immediate impulse is to reply defensively, justify your actions, and perhaps lash out. Instead of acting on this impulse, give yourself a set period – say, 30 minutes to an hour – to let the initial wave of emotion subside. During this time, instead of dwelling on the email, engage in a grounding activity to help stabilize your emotions, such as holding an ice cube in your hand or splashing cold water on your face. This physical action stimulates the vagus nerve, which plays a key role in calming down the body's fight-or-flight response. The cold sensation activates this nerve, helping to reduce the release of stress hormones like adrenaline and cortisol.

○ Rational Processing: As you allow time for your emotions to settle, your prefrontal cortex – the part of the brain responsible for rational thinking – begins to come back online. This biological shift provides a momentary pause from the emotional turmoil, enabling you to approach the situation with a calmer, more rational mindset.

○ Crafting a Measured Response: When you feel calmer and

more collected, revisit the email. With a clearer mind, you can formulate a response that is thoughtful and measured, rather than reactive.

5. Taking Action When Inclined to Withdraw

- For individuals who typically respond to triggers by withdrawing, shutting down, or avoiding, it's crucial to practice the opposite action. This means consciously choosing to engage rather than retreat.

- Example of Active Response: If you receive a challenging email from your boss and your instinct is to avoid addressing it, push yourself to respond, even with a simple message like, "I need some time to consider this, I'll get back to you soon." This action acknowledges the situation and gives you control over the timing of your response.

- Communication as a Key Tool: Similarly, in personal relationships, if something your friend or partner does triggers you, and you feel like withdrawing, communicate this to them. Let them know you're processing something and will discuss it later.

- Engage in physical actions to prevent the automatic response of shutting down. Physical activities like moderate exercise, using grounding techniques, or even vocal exercise (like humming or singing) can stimulate the vagus nerve. This stimulation helps bring you out of the withdrawal state, encourages emotional re-engagement, and fosters a more balanced physiological state.

6. Link the Trigger

- Pause to consider how the current situation is reminiscent of past childhood experiences. Example: If your partner's actions inadvertently remind you of how your parents behaved, your emotional response might be more about past trauma than the present incident.

- Recognize that your amygdala, the emotional processing center in your brain, often links current emotions to past traumas. This connection can lead to the projection of intense emotions that were originally felt towards a parent or caregiver in the past onto your partner in the present. Whether your reaction is to become overly assertive or to completely withdraw, both are forms of the same protection mechanism stemming from unresolved childhood issues.

- Ask yourself, "What does this situation remind me of from my childhood?" Actively thinking about the origin of your triggers helps in separating past emotions from the current situation, allowing for a more measured response.

7. Recognizing Safety in the Present:

- Acknowledge that rational thinking, facilitated by the prefrontal lobes, can help balance the emotional reaction from the limbic system. This mental 'teeter-totter' plays a crucial role in managing triggers.

- Differentiate this process from anxious or scattered thinking. Instead, focus on mindful, purposeful thinking to separate past experiences from present situations.

- Reflet on how current figures in your life (like your partner or boss) differ from those in your past who contributed to your trauma. For example, consider how your partner is more understanding than a parent was, or how your boss's management style differs from a parent's behavior.

- Even in moments of frustration, try to recognize positive traits or the safety provided by these individuals in your life. This practice helps in shutting off the 'emotional smoke detector' that is often overly sensitive due to past traumas.

- Realize that you now have more control and options than you did in your past. You have the ability to leave situations, express your opinions, or make significant changes, which is a significant difference from when you were a child under the influence of others.

- Understand that acknowledging and working on your triggers is a sign of emotional growth. Unlike in the past, when your parents might not have recognized their emotional triggers, you are actively seeking healthier responses and emotional understanding.

CAN TRIGGERS CHANGE OR EVOLVE?

The evolution of triggers in individuals who have experienced childhood trauma is an area of ongoing research and interest. The dynamic nature of the human brain and its capacity for change suggests that triggers can indeed evolve over time.

THE CHANGING BRAIN

1. Neuroplasticity: The brain's ability to reorganize itself, known as neuroplasticity, plays a key role in how triggers can change. As individuals grow and encounter new experiences, their brain's response to certain stimuli can evolve. This means that a trigger that once elicited a strong response may diminish over time or even cease to be a trigger.

2. Therapeutic Intervention: Engagement in therapy can significantly alter how triggers are perceived and processed. Therapies like CBT and EMDR can reframe the context of traumatic memories, potentially changing the impact of certain triggers.

DEVELOPMENTAL FACTORS

1. Age and Maturity: As individuals grow older, their cognitive and emotional capacities develop, allowing them to process and understand their trauma differently. This maturity can alter the significance of certain triggers.

2. Changing Life Circumstances: Changes in one's life situation, environment, or relationships can also influence the nature of triggers. For instance, a trigger associated with a particular place may lose its impact if the individual moves away from that environment.

THE ROLE OF NEW EXPERIENCES

1. Counter Conditioning: Positive or neutral experiences associated with previously triggering stimuli can gradually diminish the trigger's power. This process, known as counter-conditioning, involves the gradual transformation of the emotional response to a trigger.

2. Formation of New Associations: New life experiences can lead

to the formation of new associations, which can either replace old triggers or create new ones. For instance, if a previously triggering song is played in a positive context repeatedly, it may lose its association with the trauma.

Triggers related to childhood trauma are not static. They can evolve due to neuroplasticity, therapeutic interventions, developmental changes, new experiences, and ongoing stressors. This understanding underscores the importance of continuous support and therapy for individuals dealing with trauma, as their needs and responses may change over time.

Is it Possible to Completely Overcome Certain Triggers?

Research on overcoming triggers from childhood trauma is complex and multifaceted. Studies in this field have not explicitly concluded that triggers can be completely overcome. However, they do indicate that with appropriate interventions and support, individuals can significantly manage and reduce the impact of these triggers. Therapeutic approaches such as CBT, EMDR, and somatic experiences have shown effectiveness in helping individuals process and cope with their trauma. These therapies can alter how the brain responds to triggers, potentially diminishing their intensity over time. Additionally, ongoing support, mindfulness practices, and lifestyle changes can contribute to a gradual reduction in the power of these triggers. The goal of therapy and support is often to help individuals develop resilience and coping strategies rather than completely eliminate triggers, as the way trauma impacts each individual varies greatly.

Chapter Summary

- Triggers Defined: Triggers are stimuli linked to past trauma, evoking strong emotional and physiological responses.

- Brain's Role in Sensory Triggers: Sensory experiences related to trauma can reactivate the amygdala and hippocampus, causing emotional and physiological responses similar to the original trauma.

- Implicit Memory Influence: Implicit memories, which operate without conscious awareness, can influence current behaviors and emotions due to past trauma.

- Polyvagal Theory's Insight: This theory elucidates how the autonomic nervous system's varied responses to trauma shape our behaviors, offering a deeper understanding of emotional and physiological reactions stemming from childhood trauma.

- Microtriggers and Digital Influence: This section highlights the subtle yet cumulative effects of minor triggers and the significant role digital interactions play in reactivating trauma responses, emphasizing the need for awareness in digital spaces.

APPLY IT!

Journal Prompts

1. Sensory Triggers Reflection: Write about a time when a sensory experience, like a sound or smell, unexpectedly evoked a strong emotional response. Reflect on how this might connect to past trauma.

2. Exploring Implicit Memories: Consider an instance where your reaction felt disproportionate to the situation. Explore any underlying implicit memories fro your childhood that may have influenced this reaction.

3. Polyvagal Theory Insights: Consider a recent instance where you felt overwhelmed. Did you experience a 'fight, flight, freeze, or fawn' response? Reflect on how this might relate to your past experiences.

4. Identifying Microtriggers: Think about your daily routine and identify any small, repeated stressors (microtriggers) that might be impacting you. How do these accumulate and affect your mood or stress levels?

5. Digital Media Triggers: Think about your interactions with digital media and social platforms. Identify any content or interactions that may have triggered a trauma response and explore why.

Suggested Goals

1. Trigger Identification Goal: Maintain a regular journaling routine to track emotional and physical responses to daily events, helping identify and understand personal triggers.

2. Emotional Regulation Goal: Learn and practice stress management techniques to mitigate the cumulative effects of microtriggers on your well-being.

3. Education and Learning Goal: Dedicate time each week to learn more about the impact of trauma on the brain, triggers, and coping strategies. This could involve reading books, attending workshops, or participating in online courses.

4. Therapeutic Exploration: Engage in therapy sessions focusing on exploring implicit memories and their impact on your current reactions and behaviors.

5. Complete the exercises in Chapter 5 of the *Childhood Trauma and Recovery Workbook* to deepen your understanding and apply the concepts discussed.

6

Who is My Inner Child and Why Do They Need Me?

Rediscovering the Child Within

"To give the child within a voice is the most healing thing we can do for ourselves and society." – John Bradshaw

I n the journey of self-discovery and emotional healing, understanding the concept of the inner child is pivotal. The inner child is not merely a metaphorical entity; it's a profound psychological reality that inhabits the depths of our psyche. This chapter examines the intricate nature of the inner child, exploring its definition, origins, and the crucial role it plays in our adult lives.

At its core, the inner child embodies the cumulative emotional experiences and memories of our childhood, stored within the subconscious. This aspect of ourselves holds onto the innocence, creativity, and wonder of childhood, yet it also bears the scars of any trauma, neglect, or unmet needs we experience. The concept, deeply rooted in psychotherapy and personal growth disciplines, suggests that this childlike part of us continues to influence our adult behaviors, emotions, and even our relationships.

Tracing back to the work of Carl Jung and his theories of archetypes, the inner child is seen as a universal symbol of renewal and potential growth. It's an archetype representing our most primal emotions and experiences from our earliest years. The evolution of this concept through Object Relations Theory and the significant contributions of figures like D.W. Winnicott and John Bradshaw have shed light on how our early interactions and environment shape our true selves, including this childlike aspect.

In contemporary therapeutic practices, the inner child is more than just a concept; it's a gateway to healing and understanding. By reconnecting with this part of ourselves, we uncover the emotional importings of our childhood and begin to address the unresolved traumas or needs that linger into adulthood. This reconnection is not only about revisiting past pains but also about rediscovering the joy, spontaneity, and pure emotion that the inner child represents.

This chapter will guide you through the significance of the inner child in the context of trauma recovery, emphasizing how early experiences cast long shadows over our adult lives. It will explore various perspectives and research on the subject, underlining the therapeutic value of nurturing and healing the inner child. You will understand why your inner child needs you – for comfort, resolution, and ultimately, for a more integrated, authentic, and emotionally healthy adult life.

Through this exploration, we will uncover the various manifestations of the inner child in adult behavior and emotions. By recognizing these signs, you can begin the journey of meeting your inner child's needs and healing the wounds that have been carried, often unknowingly, for so long. The chapter will provide insights into the challenges and rewards of this journey, equipping you with the understanding necessary to embrace and nurture your inner child.

INTRODUCTION TO THE INNER CHILD CONCEPT

DEFINITION AND ORIGINS

The concept of the 'inner child' is a metaphorical representation of an individual's childlike aspect. It refers to the part of one's psyche that retains innocence, creativity, awe, and wonder towards life.

Psychologically, it embodies the cumulative emotional experiences and memories stored in the subconscious from childhood.

This concept, often used in psychotherapy and personal growth, posits that everyone carries their childhood self within their adult persona. The inner child can manifest in various forms of behaviors and emotional states, especially those deeply rooted in early life experiences.

HISTORICAL ORIGINS AND THEORETICAL BACKGROUND

1. Carl Jung's Archetypes: The origins of the inner child concept can be traced back to Carl Jung's theories. Jung, a Swiss psychiatrist and psychoanalyst, introduced the idea of archetypes, which are universal, archaic symbols and images that derive from the collective unconscious. The 'child archetype,' as proposed by Jung, symbolizes renewal, rebirth, and growth potential, pivotal elements of the inner child.

2. Object Relations Theory: This concept was further developed in the context of Object Relations Theory, a psychoanalytic theory that emphasizes the importance of early relationships and the environment in the development of the self. Experts in this field, like D.W. Winnicott, postulated that the true self, including the childlike aspects, is shaped by early interactions with primary caregivers.

3. John Bradshaw's Contribution: Psychologist John Bradshaw popularized the concept of the inner child in mainstream psychology during the late 20th century, particularly in the 1980s and 1990s. He emphasized the significance of nurturing and healing the inner child for emotional well-being and recovery from past traumas. Bradshaw's work brought the concept into therapeutic practice, especially in the treatment of codependency, addiction, and dysfunctional family systems.

THE INNER CHILD IN MODERN THERAPY

Contemporary therapeutic approaches, such as CBT and Gestalt Therapy (discussed more later), incorporate inner child work to help individuals reconnect with and heal their childlike aspects. This work often involves revisiting childhood experiences, understanding their impact on the present, and addressing unresolved emotional needs or traumas.

INFLUENCE OF EARLY CHILDHOOD EXPERIENCES

Academic research and case studies have consistently shown the profound impact of early childhood experiences on adult mental health. Experts in developmental psychology assert that unresolved childhood trauma, neglect, or unmet emotional needs can lead to various psychological issues in adulthood, making the concept of the inner child particularly relevant in therapy.

The inner child concept serves as a valuable tool in understanding and addressing deep-rooted emotional issues stemming from childhood. Its origins from Jungian archetypes to modern psychotherapy reflect an evolving understanding of human psychology. By acknowledging and nurturing the inner child, therapeutic practices aim to foster emotional healing and personal growth.

RELEVANCE IN TRAUMA RECOVERY

THE ROLE OF THE INNER CHILD IN TRAUMA RECOVERY

Understanding the inner child concept is crucial in the context of trauma recovery. This section explores the relevance of the inner child in healing from traumatic childhood experiences.

1. Trauma and the Inner Child: Trauma experienced in childhood often leaves lasting impressions on the inner child. The unresolved emotions and memories connected to these traumas can continue to influence an individual's emotional and psychological state in adulthood. Addressing these aspects is vital in the therapeutic process.

2. Reconnecting with the Inner Child: Engaging with the inner child allows adults to access and process emotions that have been suppressed since childhood. This process can lead to significant breakthroughs in trauma recovery, as it helps individuals confront and make sense of their past experiences.

3. Experts on Trauma and the Inner Child: Renowned trauma

experts such as Dr. Bessel van der Kolk and Dr. Peter Levine have emphasized the importance of acknowledging and healing the inner child in their therapeutic approaches. Their research indicates that many symptoms of trauma, including dissociation, hyperarousal, and avoidance, can be linked to unresolved issues from childhood.

Evidence from Case Studies and Research

1. Therapeutic Case Studies: Numerous case studies in psychotherapy literature document the effectiveness of inner child work in trauma recovery. Patients who engage with their inner child often report a great sense of closure, emotional release, and understanding of their trauma.

2. Academic Research: Research published in journals such as the *Journal of Trauma & Dissociation* and *Clinical Psychology Review* supports the therapeutic value of inner child work. These studies show how reconnecting with and nurturing the inner child can lead to improved mental health outcomes for trauma survivors.

The inner child concept plays a pivotal role in trauma recovery. By acknowledging and nurturing the inner child, individuals can heal from the deep-seated impacts of childhood trauma. The integration of this concept into therapeutic practices has been supported by a wealth of research and expert opinion, underscoring its importance in effective trauma treatment.

The Role of the Inner Child in Adult Life

The concept of the inner child is pivotal in adult life, influencing behaviors, emotions, and interpersonal relationships. This internal childlike aspect, shaped by early experiences, continues to impact individuals into adulthood. The inner child often manifests in adult emotional responses, with intense reactions such as anger, fear, or sadness sometimes stemming from the inner child reacting to situations that mirror past traumas or unmet needs. Similarly, adults might engage in behavioral patterns echoing their childhood experiences, like people-pleasing or conflict avoidance, which are learned behaviors from the inner child aimed at gaining approval or avoiding distress.

In interpersonal relationships, the inner child significantly influences one's attachment style, with early experiences with caregivers shaping perceptions and responses to intimacy and dependency. Conflicts in adult relationships can trigger the inner child, leading to defensive or regressive communication styles, which underscores the importance of recognizing these triggers for healthy conflict resolution.

Unresolved childhood trauma can lead to the reenactment of past dynamics in adult life, where the inner child, still grappling with past hurts, unconsciously seeks out similar situations or relationships. Adults often develop coping mechanisms that originated as strategies the inner child created to manage distress or instability. Acknowledging and validating the inner child is the first step in healing, leading to a deeper understanding of one's emotional and behavioral patterns. Engaging in playful and creative activities can provide a therapeutic channel for the inner child to express itself, reconnecting with aspects of joy, wonder, and spontaneity.

Inner child work is a powerful tool in self-discovery and personal growth, allowing individuals to explore and heal the deepest parts of themselves, leading to greater self-awareness and authenticity. By addressing the inner child's unmet needs and unresolved traumas, adults can develop greater emotional resilience, robust coping strategies, and improved emotional regulation. Understanding and nurturing the inner child is crucial for resolving past traumas and promoting emotional well-being and personal growth, leading to a more integrated and fulfilled sense of se lf.

IMPACT ON BEHAVIOR AND EMOTIONS

Drawing upon the pioneering work of John Bradshaw, it becomes clear that the inner child exerts a significant influence on adult behavior. Bradshaw's research and writings, particularly in *Homecoming: Reclaiming and Healing Your Inner Child*, illuminate how behaviors in our adult lives often stem from unresolved childhood experiences. For instance, patterns such as avoiding intimacy or displaying overly controlling behaviors can be traced back to coping mechanisms developed in response to early family dynamics. These behaviors are manifestations of the inner child's attempts to navigate through and adapt to the emotional landscape of their upbringing.

Bradshaw's concept of the inner child also profoundly impacts emotional responses in adulthood. He elucidates how emotions like unexplained sadness, outbursts of anger, or deep-seated fears often have their origins in the unaddressed emotional needs or traumas experienced in childhood. Adults may find themselves experiencing intense emotional reactions to situations that, on the surface, seem unrelated to these past experiences. However, these reactions are the inner child's response to stimuli that unconsciously trigger past wounds.

Bradshaw's work also examines the influence of the inner child on adult relationships. He highlights how early attachment styles, shaped by interactions with caregivers, inform the way adults engage in relationships. For example, an adult exhibiting anxious attachment behaviors in relationships might be echoing the inner child's experiences of inconsistent caregiving. These deeply ingrained patterns, if unaddressed, continue to play out in adult relationships, often replicating the emotional environment of the individual's childhood.

Bradshaw provides several examples to illustrate these dynamics:

1. Relationship Dynamics: Adults who experienced abandonment or neglect in childhood may develop patterns of clinginess or emotional withdrawal in relationships, reflecting a continuous search for validation or a protective mechanism against potential abandonment.

2. Self-Esteem Issues: Constant criticism or feeling inadequate in childhood can lead to chronic low self-esteem in adults. This often results in perfectionism or achievement-seeking behaviors as adults strive for external validation.

3. Control and Rigidity: Growing up in chaotic environments might lead adults to develop a heightened need for control and predictability, manifesting as rigidity in routines or a reluctance to embrace change.

4. Substance Abuse and Addictive Behaviors: Bradshaw links childhood trauma to the development of addictive behaviors in adulthood, where substances or compulsive behaviors become coping mechanisms for numbing unresolved childhood pain.

5. Emotional Dysregulation: Adults with unresolved childhood trauma might experience difficulty regulating their emotions, leading to mood swings, sudden anger outbursts, or an inability to cope with stress.

6. Fear of Abandonment: Experiencing loss or abandonment as a child can lead to a persistent fear of abandonment in adulthood. This fear often results in unstable relationships, either through excessive clinging or pushing others away to pre-empt perceived abandonment.

In conclusion, Bradshaw's work provides a comprehensive understanding of the inner child's significant role in shaping adult behavior and emotional responses. By addressing the needs and experiences of the inner child, adults can alter maladaptive patterns and achieve greater emotional maturity. His examples and theoretical framework emphasize the importance of inner child work in personal growth and emotional healing, offering a nuanced perspective on the diverse manifestations of the inner child in adult life.

Examples of Inner Child Manifestations

Further examples of inner child manifestations in adults, drawn from both clinical observations and psychological theories, provide insight into how unresolved childhood experiences and emotions continue to influence behavior and emotional responses in adulthood. Here are some notable examples, including some unique ones that highlight the diverse ways the inner child can influence adult behavior and emotions:

1. Spontaneous Joy and Wonder: Adults displaying an uninhibited sense of joy and wonder, often in simple or everyday situations, can be a positive manifestation of the inner child. This reflects a preserved sense of innocence and the ability to find delight in the world.

2. Fear of Authority Figures: An adult who disproportionately fears authority figures or feels overly submissive in their presence may be manifesting an inner child's response to authoritarian parents or caregivers from their childhood.

3. Resistance to Structure or Discipline: Some adults might show a strong resistance to structured environments or discipline, which can be linked to the inner child's response to overly rigid or controlling childhood experiences.

4. Need for Validation and Approval: Constantly seeking validation and approval from others can be a manifestation of the inner child's unmet need for acknowledgment and praise during formative years.

5. Rebellious or Contrarian Behavior: Adults who often exhibit rebellious or contrarian behaviors, even in inconsequential situations, might be expressing their inner child's desire to assert autonomy that was suppressed in childhood.

6. Challenges with Financial Responsibility: Difficulties in managing

finances responsibly can sometimes be traced back to the inner child's unmet needs or a lack of proper modeling in financial responsibility during childhood.

7. Attachment to Physical Objects: A strong emotional attachment to physical objects, especially those without apparent significant value, can be an expression of the inner child holding onto memories or seeking comfort in familiarity.

8. Overwhelming Fear of Failure: An adult who experiences intense fear of failure or exhibits extreme risk-avoidance behavior may be manifesting the inner child's fear of criticism or failure experienced during childhood.

9. Subconscious Self-Sabotage: The inner child might influence adults to engage in self-sabotage, especially if they internalized negative beliefs about themselves during childhood. This can manifest in various aspects of life, including careers, relationships, and personal growth.

10. Perfectionism and High Self-Expectations: Adults might exhibit perfectionism or set unrealistically high standards for themselves, often driven by an inner child's desire to be accepted, loved, or praised, which they might not have adequately received in childhood.

11. Impulse Control Issues: Difficulty in controlling impulses can sometimes be traced back to the inner child's unmet needs for attention and care. This can manifest as impulsive decision-making or behaviors that seek immediate gratification.

12. Nurturing and Caretaking Behaviors: Some adults might excessively nurture or take care of others, often neglecting their own needs. This can stem from the inner child's desire to create the security and care they craved in their own childhood.

These examples illustrate the varied and complex ways in which the inner child can manifest in adult behavior and emotional responses. They highlight the enduring impact of childhood experiences and the importance of addressing these aspects for emotional well-being and personal growth.

COMMON INNER CHILD WOUNDS

The concept of inner child wounds refers to deep emotional hurts experienced during childhood that continue to impact an individual's life into adulthood. These sounds, often formed in response to traumatic or neglectful experiences, manifest in various ways. This subchapter explores the most common inner child wounds, providing insight into their origins and effects.

1. Abandonment Wounds: These wounds arise when a child feels left alone, uncared for, or unloved, whether physically or emotionally. Adults carrying abandonment wounds may struggle with fears of being left in relationships, leading to clinginess or a pattern of staying in unhealthy relationships.

2. Neglect Wounds: Emotional or physical neglect in childhood can lead to inner child wounds characterized by feelings of worthlessness or being invisible. In adulthood, these wounds might manifest as a tendency to neglect one's own needs or believe that one's needs and feelings are unimportant.

3. Trust Wounds: These wounds develop when a child's trust is repeatedly broken, whether through betrayal, inconsistency, or deception. Adults with trust wounds often have difficulty trusting others, leading to challenges in forming deep and secure relationships.

4. Guilt and Shame Wounds: Children who were frequently blamed, criticized, or made to feel guilty can develop these wounds. As adults, they might struggle with excessive guilt, a lack of self-worth, or a deep-seated feeling of being inherently flawed or bad.

5. Authority Wounds: Children who grew up in overly rigid or authoritarian environments may develop authority wounds. This can result in adults who either rebel against all forms of authority or, conversely, are overly submissive and struggle to assert themselves.

6. Trauma Wounds: Trauma wounds result from experiencing or witnessing traumatic events in childhood. They can lead to various mental health issues in adulthood, including PTSD, anxiety, and depression.

ARCHETYPES OF THE WOUNDED INNER CHILD

UNDERSTANDING ARCHETYPES OF THE WOUNDED INNER CHILD

The concept of the wounded inner child can manifest in various archetypical forms, each representing different aspects of childhood pain and trauma. These archetypes help in understanding the specific ways childhood wounds continue to influence adult behavior and emotions. This subchapter explores the most common archetypes of the wounded inner child, providing a framework for recognizing and addressing these deep-seated emotional injuries.

KEY ARCHETYPES OF THE WOUNDED INNER CHILD

THE ABANDONED CHILD

Drawing from Carl Jung's work on archetypes, the Abandoned Child archetype embodies a profound aspect of the human psyche, resonating deeply with those who have experienced abandonment in their formative years. This archetype is characterized by an inherent fear of being left alone, a reflection of the universal human experience of abandonment. It manifests in a pervasive longing for connection and security, stemming from unmet needs during childhood. Individuals resonating with this archetype often exhibit heightened vulnerability and emotional sensitivity, indicative of the deep emotional wounds sustained through abandonment.

In adult behavior and relationships, the influence of the Abandoned Child archetype is evident in the development of anxious or avoidant attachment styles. These patterns are rooted in underlying fears of abandonment and a need for reassurance. Jung's concepts of projection and transference are particularly relevant, as adults might project their abandonment fears onto their relationships, interpreting interactions through the lens of their deep-seated insecurities. Moreover, the symbolism and imagery in dreams, a key aspect of Jungian analysis, often reflect the inner turmoil and pain associated with this archetype.

Healing the Abandoned Child archetype in Jungian therapy involves confronting and integrating this aspect into one's conscious understanding. Techniques like active imagination and dream analysis are employed to explore and heal the archetype, allowing individuals to engage with and understand the symbolic expressions of their inner fears and needs. The therapeutic goal is to develop a more secure internal foundation, reducing external dependency and fostering self-reliance and inner stability. This approach helps in addressing the root causes of abandonment issues, leading to emotional healing and the development of more secure and fulfilling adult relationships.

Through the Jungian lens, the Abandoned Child archetype provides key insights into the experiences and healing processes of those who have faced childhood abandonment. It underscores the universal nature of this experience and highlights the importance of acknowledging and integrating this archetype for comprehensive emotional healing and personal growth.

THE NEGLECTED CHILD

Drawing from the principles of psychology and the understanding of inner child dynamics, the Neglected Child archetype represents individuals who, in their formative years, experienced a lack of attention, care, or emotional support. This archetype is not just a personal experience but a reflection of a broader human condition where emotional or physical neglect during childhood leaves a lasting impact on the psyche. Adults embodying this archetype often carry a profound sense of worthlessness or invisibility, having internalized the feeling of being overlooked or unimportant during their early years.

In adult life, the Neglected Child archetype manifests in various ways. Such individuals may neglect their own needs, having learned to deprioritize themselves due to the lack of attention they received as children. They might also continuously seek external validation, driven by an unresolved need for acknowledgment and recognition. This ongoing search for validation often stems from their childhood experiences of feeling unseen and unheard.

The healing process for those identified with the Neglected Child archetype involves recognizing and addressing these deep-seated emotional wounds. Therapeutic interventions often focus on helping individuals acknowledge and tend to their neglected needs. By doing so, they can begin to establish a sense of self-worth that is independent of external validation. The journey of healing the Neglected Child involves learning to value oneself, cultivating self-care practices, and developing a healthy level of self-esteem.

Understanding and addressing the needs of the Neglected Child archetype is crucial for emotional growth and well-being. It allows individuals to move beyond the patterns of neglect and invisibility that have shaped their lives, leading to a more fulfilling and self-affirming existence. This process is key to breaking the cycle of neglect and fostering a sense of self that is grounded in self-respect and self-recognition.

THE BETRAYED CHILD

The Betrayed Child archetype emerges from experiences of betrayal, broken trust, or deception in childhood, leaving a profound impact on an individual's ability to trust and form secure relationships in adulthood. This archetype symbolizes the deep emotional scars resulting from instances where a child's trust was violated, whether through unkept promises, dishonesty, or betrayal by primary caregivers or close family members. The pain and confusion stemming from these early betrayals often set the template for how these individuals navigate trust and intimacy later in life.

Adults who resonate with the Betrayed Child archetype may exhibit a pervasive wariness or skepticism in their relationships. They often find it challenging to trust others fully, harboring a fear that they will be betrayed again. This lack of trust can manifest as reluctance to open up emotionally, resistance to forming deep connections, or a tendency to question the motives of others, even in the absence of any real threat of betrayal. In some cases, this archetype can lead to self-protective behaviors where individuals preemptively distance themselves from others as a way to avoid potential hurt.

The healing journey for those identified with the Betrayed Child archetype involves working through these deeply ingrained trust issues. If often requires rebuilding a sense of safety and learning to discern trustworthy behaviors in others. Therapeutic work may focus on processing the original betrayal experiences, understanding their impact, and developing new, healthier patterns of trust. Key to this process is learning to recognize that past betrayals do not have to dictate future relationships.

Addressing the needs of the Betrayed Child archetype is critical for emotional healing and the development of healthy, trusting relationships.It enables individuals to move beyond the protective walls built in response to early betrayals and to engage more openly and vulnerably with the world. This path of healing fosters resilience and the ability to form deeper, more meaningful connections with others.

THE VICTIM CHILD

The Victim Child archetype represents individuals who, in their formative years, experience situations where they feel powerless, victimized, or helpless. This archetype stems from childhood circumstances where the individual might have been subjected to bullying, abuse, or neglect, leading to a deep-seated sense of victimhood that persists into adulthood. The core of the Victim Child archetype is learned helplessness, where the child internalizes the belief that they are perpetually at the mercy of others or circumstances.

In adulthood, those who resonate with the Victim Child archetype often exhibit a mindset where they see themselves as perpetual victims. They might struggle with self-empowerment and often feel that life is happening to them, rather than seeing themselves as active agents. This can manifest in a tendency to blame external factors for personal challenges, difficulties in taking initiative, or a general sense of passivity in facing life's hurdles. Adults embodying this archetype might also find themselves repeatedly in situations where they feel victimized, reinforcing their ingrained belief system.

Healing the Victim Child archetype involves a journey of reclaiming personal power and shifting the narrative from one of victimhood to one of resilience and agency. Therapeutic work often focuses on helping individuals recognize and break the cycle of victimization. This process includes building self-efficacy, learning to assert boundaries, and developing a more proactive approach to life's challenges.

Therapists may use various techniques, such as CBT to challenge and change victim-oriented thought patterns, or narrative therapy to help individuals reframe their life stories in a more empowering way. Key to healing the Victim Child is fostering a sense of inner strength and resilience, enabling individuals to move beyond the past experiences of victimization and embrace a more empowered and active role in their lives.

Addressing the Victim Child archetype is vital for emotional growth and well-being. It allows individuals to shed the restrictive identity of a victim and step into a more empowered and self-determined life, marked by personal strength and a proactive approach to challenges.

THE INVISIBLE CHILD

The Invisible Child archetype arises from childhood experiences where a child feels unseen, unheard, or overlooked, often in environments where their emotional or physical presence is consistently ignored or minimized. This archetype embodies the feelings of neglect and invisibility experienced by children who may have grown up in families where caregivers were emotionally unavailable, preoccupied, or focused on other family issues. As a result, these children learn to suppress their needs, emotions, and expressions, adapting to their environment by becoming 'invisible.'

In adulthood, individuals resonating with the Invisible Child archetype might struggle with self-expression and assertiveness. They often feel overlooked or undervalued in social situations, workplaces, and relationships. This can manifest as a reluctance to voice opinions, a tendency to blend into the background, or difficulty in asserting their needs and boundaries. Adults embodying this archetype might also find it challenging to recognize and honor their worth, having internalized the belief that they do not deserve attention or acknowledgment.

Healing the Invisible Child involves a process of reclaiming visibility and voice. Therapeutic approaches may focus on helping individuals recognize their value and develop the confidence to express themselves. Techqnies like assertiveness training, self-esteem building exercises, and narrative therapy can be effective in addressing the deep-seated feelings of invisibility. A significant aspect of this healing journey is learning to acknowledge and attend to one's own needs, desires, and emotions, which were neglected during childhood.

Therapists might also encourage creative expressions such as art, writing, or drama, which can provide outlets for the invisible child to be seen and heard. The goal is to create a safe space where the individual can explore and express their true self without fear of being ignored or dismissed.

Addressing the needs of the Invisible Child archetype is crucial for fostering a sense of self-worth and belonging. It enables individuals to step out of the shadows of their childhood invisibility and engage more fully and authentically with the world around them. This process is key to overcoming the legacy of feeling unseen and building a life where they feel recognized, valued, and empowered.

THE SCAPEGOAT CHILD

The Scapegoat Child archetype emerges from experiences in childhood where a child is unfairly blamed, criticized, or made responsible for family problems. This archetype is typically formed in family dynamics where a child is designated, either overly or subtly, as the cause of dysfunction or conflict, leading to feelings of guilt and inadequacy. The scapegoat often bears the burden of family issues, becoming a receptacle for negative emotions and blame.

Adults who identify with the Scapegoat Child archetype may carry into their adult life a deep-seated sense of being at fault or the root cause of problems, even when such beliefs are unwarranted. This can manifest as a propensity to assume responsibility for issues beyond their control, a persistent feeling of guilt, or a belief that they are inherently flawed. Such individuals might also find themselves repeatedly in situations where they are blamed or targeted, perpetuating the role of the scapegoat that was assigned to them in childhood.

Healing the scapegoat Child involves challenging and reshaping these ingrained beliefs of guilt and unworthiness. Therapeutic interventions might focus on helping individuals understand the dynamics of their childhood environment and recognize that the role of the scapegoat was unfairly imposed upon them. Therapies like family systems therapy can be particularly effective in exploring and addressing these dynamics.

Part of the healing process includes learning to differentiate between taking healthy responsibility and being inappropriately blamed. Developing self-compassion, setting boundaries, and cultivating a supportive network are crucial steps in overcoming the scapegoat mentality. Individuals may also benefit from practices that reinforce their self-worth and help them recognize their strengths and values outside of being a scapegoat.

Addressing the Scapegoad Child archetype is essential for individuals to break free from the patterns of blame and criticism that have overshadowed their lives. It allows them to redefine their identity, moving beyond the unjust role of the scapegoat to a place of self-empowerment and authentic self-expression. This journey is key to overcoming the negative impacts of being scapegoated and building a more positive and self-affirming life.

WHY YOUR INNER CHILD NEEDS YOU

Your inner child needs you because it represents the emotional and psychological state of your childhood self, carrying the needs, wounds, and experiences from that crucial developmental period. Here's why attending to your inner child is essential:

1. Healing Emotional Wounds: Your inner child may hold onto emotional wounds from the past, such as feelings of abandonment, neglect, or trauma. As an adult, you have the awareness, resources, and capacity to provide the care, validation, and healing that your inner child didn't receive at the t ime.

2. Resolving Unfinished Business: Childhood experiences often leave unresolved issues that can influence your current behavior and emotional well-being. By nurturing your inner child, you address these unresolved aspects, allowing for a more integrated and healthier adult life.

3. Emotional Regulation: Your inner child's unmet needs can manifest in your adult life as emotional dysregulation, anxiety, depression, or relationship issues. Recognizing and meeting these needs can lead to better emotional balance and improved mental health.

4. Unlocking Creativity and Joy: The inner child is also a source of creativity, spontaneity, and joy. Engaging with your inner child can reignite these qualities, enhancing your life with renewed energy and creativity.

5. Improving Self-Awareness: Understanding your inner child allows for deeper self-awareness. It helps you understand the root causes of your fears, desires, and motivations, leading to more conscious and fulfilling life choices.

6. Enhancing Relationships: Many relationship challenges stem from unmet childhood needs. By healing your inner child, you can develop healthier relationship patterns and more profound connections with others.

7. Breaking Cycles: If you've experienced negative family patterns or trauma, attending to your inner child can prevent the continuation of these cycles, especially if you have or plan to have children.

8. Fostering Self-Compassion: Nurturing your inner child cultivates self-compassion. It's a process of learning to treat yourself with the same kindness, care, and understanding that you would offer a child.

Your inner child represents the most vulnerable and authentic part of you. It holds the key to understanding and healing your deepest emotional wounds and plays a crucial role in your overall emotional and psychological well-being. By nurturing your inner child, you acknowledge and attend to these vital aspects of yourself, paving the way for a more balanced, joyful, and fulfilling life.

RECOGNIZING THE INNER CHILD'S NEEDS

Determining what your inner child needs involves a process of introspection and awareness, often guided by recognizing certain emotional and behavioral patterns that stem from childhood experiences. Here are some ways to uncover what your inner child might need:

1. Reflect on Childhood Experiences: Start by reflecting on your childhood. Think about experiences that were particularly impactful, both positively and negatively. Consider what emotions or needs were present in those moments. For instance, moments of fear or loneliness might indicate a need for safety and comfort.

2. Identity Recurrent Emotional Themes: Pay attention to recurring emotional themes in your life. Do you often feel abandoned, neglected, or unworthy? Such feelings can be clues to what your inner child is still seeking or lacking.

3. Notice Triggers and Reactions: Observe situations that trigger strong emotional reactions. These reactions can be disproportionate to the present situation but make sense in the context of your childhood. For example, if criticism makes you overly upset, your inner child might need validation and support.

4. Journaling and Self-Exploration: Keeping a journal can be a useful tool for exploring your inner child's needs. Write about your feelings, reactions, and any memories that come up. Over time, patterns may emerge that point to specific needs.

5. Therapeutic Guidance: A therapist, especially one skilled in inner child work, can help you identify and understand your inner child's needs. They can provide tools and techniques for exploring your childhood and current emotional landscape.

6. Dream Analysis: Sometimes, the inner child communicates through dreams. Analyzing your dreams for symbols or themes

related to childhood can provide insights into your inner child's needs.

7. Body Awareness: Pay attention to physical sensations and responses. The body often holds emotional memories, and physical discomfort or tension can indicate unresolved emotional issues from childhood.

8. Creative Expression: Engaging in creative activities like art, music, or dance can help express and explore emotions related to the inner child. These activities can be particularly revealing of your deeper feelings and needs.

9. Mindfulness and Meditation: Practices like mindfulness and meditation can help you become more attuned to your inner emotional state, allowing you to connect with and understand your inner child's needs more deeply.

10. Revisiting Childhood Activities: Engaging in activities you enjoyed as a child or exploring new ones you wish you had experienced can be enlightening. It can reveal what brings joy, comfort, or a sense of fulfillment to your inner child.

By using these methods, you can start to build a clearer picture of what your inner child needs to heal and feel whole. This understanding is a vital step in your journey toward emotional healing and personal growth.

Chapter Summary

- Emotional Continuity from Childhood to Adulthood: The inner child is a crucial aspect of our psyche, representing our childhood experiences and emotions, which significantly influence our adult behavior and emotional responses.

- Healing Through Reconnection: Engaging with and nurturing our inner child is vital for healing emotional wounds and resolving unresolved issues from our childhood, leading to improved mental health and emotional regulation.

- Impact on Adult Relationships: The inner child greatly affects our adult relationships, with early childhood experiences shaping our attachment styles and influencing how we interact with others.

- Manifestations of the Inner Child: The inner child manifests in various forms in adults, including emotional overreactions, fears, and certain behaviors, which are often rooted in childhood experiences.

- Role in Personal Growth: Understanding and addressing the needs of the inner child is essential for personal growth, self-awareness, and breaking negative cycles inherited from childhood.

APPLY IT!

Journal Prompts

1. Assessing Emotional Overreactions: Reflect on a recent emotional reaction that seemed intense or disproportionate. Consider how this might relate to your inner child's needs or past experiences.

2. Revisiting Joyful Childhood Moments: Recall a happy childhood memory. What elements of this memory can you bring into your current life to nurture your inner child?

3. Connecting with Your Inner Child: Write a letter to your inner child, expressing understanding, compassion, and support for what they went through in the past.

4. Understanding Fears and Insecurities: Think about a recurring fear or insecurity. Explore how this might be connected to your childhood experiences and what your inner child might need to feel safe.

5. Changing Inner Child-Influenced Behaviors: Identify a behavior or pattern in your life that you want to change. Consider how this might be related to the unmet needs of your inner child and how addressing those needs could facilitate change.

Suggested Goals

1. Self-Reflection Goal: Dedicate time each week to reflect on your childhood experiences and how they impact your

current emotions and behaviors. This could involve journaling, meditation, or therapy.

2. Inner Child Nurturing Goal: Engage in activities that bring joy and comfort to your inner child regularly. This could be anything from creative hobbies to spending time in nature.

3. Building Emotional Awareness: Practice identifying and labeling emotions as they arise, linking them to possible childhood experiences or needs.

4. Mindfulness Practice Goal: Incorporate mindfulness practices into your daily routine to become more aware of your inner child's presence and needs. This could involve mindful breathing, body scanning, or mindful walking.

5. Self-Compassion Routine: Incorporate a daily self-compassion exercise, such as a positive affirmation or self-care activity, to nurture your inner child.

6. Complete the exercises in Chapter 6 of the *Childhood Trauma and Recovery Workbook* to deepen your understanding and apply the concepts discussed.

7

How Can I Begin to Heal My Inner Child?

STEPS TOWARD EMOTIONAL RENEWAL AND INNER CHILD HARMONY

"Caring for myself is not self-indulgence, it is self-preservation, and that is an act of political warfare." – Audre Lorde

Embarking on the journey to heal one's inner child can be a transformative and deeply rewarding experience. This journey is about reconnecting with and nurturing the part of ourselves that still experiences the emotions, traumas, and joys of childhood. It involves understanding and healing the wounds of the past to foster emotional growth and well-being in the present. In this chapter, "How Can I Begin to Heal My Inner Child?", we will explore various aspects of the healing process, providing insights and practical steps to guide you through this profound journey of self-discovery and renewal.

Healing from childhood trauma and nurturing your inner child is not a straightforward path. It's a journey filled with nuances and complexities, reflecting the unique experiences and emotional landscapes of each individual. The healing process is inherently non-linear, marked by ups and downs, breakthroughs, and setbacks. It's a journey that requires patience, understanding, and a compassionate approach to self-reflection and personal growth.

We'll dive into the therapeutic approaches that have been developed to specifically address the needs of the inner child, exploring how psychoanalytic, cognitive-behavioral, gestalt, and narrative therapies, among others, can facilitate healing. We'll also look at practical exercises for inner child work, providing tools for engaging with and understanding your inner child.

Understanding and overcoming the challenges and obstacles commonly encountered in inner child work is crucial. We will discuss strategies to navigate these challenges, helping you maintain a steady course on your healing journey. Additionally, we will address the skepticism that sometimes surrounds inner child work, offering perspectives and evidence to validate its importance and efficacy.

The chapter will also highlight inspiring case studies and success stories of inner child healing, demonstrating the transformative power of this work. These stories serve as hope and inspiration, showcasing the profound changes that can occur when individuals courageously engage with their inner child.

Lastly, we will explore the long-term benefits of healing your inner child. This healing journey, while deeply personal, has far-reaching effects on all aspects of your life, leading to enhanced emotional well-being, improved relationships, increased self-esteem, and a greater overall sense of fulfillment and joy.

Join us on this journey of healing and discovery, as we explore the multifaceted process of reconnecting with and nurturing your inner child. It's a path toward emotional liberation, self-acceptance, and profound personal growth.

THE HEALING PROCESS

The journey of healing from childhood trauma and engaging in inner child work is inherently non-linear, distinguished by its varied pace and unpredictable nature. Unlike a physical ailment that might follow a predictable healing trajectory, the emotional and psychological healing from childhood wounds can oscillate between periods of significant progress and times of seeming stagnation. This path is characterized by its cyclical nature, where individuals may find themselves revisiting old emotions or traumas multiple times, each cycle offering a deeper layer of understanding and healing.

During this process, it's not uncommon to encounter triggering events that might bring about a regression or a re-emergence of past issues. These moments are not setbacks but rather integral parts of the healing journey, providing opportunities for deeper emotional work and insight. Moreover, the translation of therapeutic breakthroughs and insights into tangible changes in one's emotional state or behavior often takes time, underscoring the gradual aspect of this journey.

Navigating this non-linear path requires a blend of patience and self-compassion. Recognizing and accepting the ebb and flow of the healing process is essential to maintain motivation and perspective. Regular self-reflection, whether through journaling, meditation, or therapy sessions, plays a crucial role in facilitating a deeper understanding of the nuances of one's emotional journey and the progress being made.

Support systems, be it therapists, support groups, or understanding friends and family, are invaluable. They provide not only an external perspective but also encouragement and empathy during more challenging phases. Celebrating small victories and acknowledging every step forward, no matter how minor it may seem, can be incredibly empowering, reinforcing a sense of progress and achievement.

Flexibility in the healing process is also key. Being open to adjusting therapeutic methods or exploring new self-help strategies can make a significant difference, especially when certain approaches do not resonate as expected This adaptability allows for a more personalized and effective healing journey.

In conclusion, the healing journey from childhood trauma and through inner child work is a deeply personal and evolving process. It transcends a linear progression, requiring an understanding of its complex, cyclical nature. Embracing this non-linearity with patience, support, and flexibility paves the way for a journey that, despite its challenges, leads to profound personal growth and healing.

Therapeutic Approaches to Healing the Inner Child

In the realm of healing from childhood trauma, various therapeutic approaches have been developed and refined to address the needs of the inner child. These methodologies, grounded in academic research, clinical case studies, and expert insights, aim to facilitate the healing of deep-rooted emotional wounds and foster personal growth. This subchapter explores some of the most effective therapeutic approaches for inner child healing.

Psychoanalytic and Psychodynamic Therapy

Psychoanalytic and psychodynamic therapies look into the unconscious mind, seeking to uncover and resolve deep-seated conflicts and traumas from childhood. These approaches, rooted in the works of Freud and later expanded by Jung, focus on understanding how early life experiences shape the adult psyche. By exploring these foundational experiences, individuals can begin to heal their inner child. Clinical studies in journals like the *International Journal of Psychoanalysis* have highlighted the efficacy of these therapies in accessing and healing deep emotional wounds.

Cognitive Behavioral Therapy (CBT) is a structured approach addressing thoughts, feelings, and behaviors interconnected with trauma. We'll explore various forms of CBT, including Traditional CBT, Trauma-Focused CBT, and Dialectical Behavior Therapy focusing on their specific roles in trauma therapy.

Narrative Therapy, developed by Michael White and David Epston, empowers individuals to rewrite their life narratives. This approach is particularly effective in externalizing trauma and re-authoring stories with resilience and strength.

Gestalt Therapy offers a holistic and experiential approach, emphasizing present awareness and the integration of life experiences. It aids individuals in recognizing the impact of past traumas on their current lives through mindfulness, experiential techniques, and creative experimentation.

Each method provides a unique perspective on understanding and healing childhood trauma, offering insights into their principles, applications, and evidence of their effectiveness in trauma treatment. This subchapter aims to guide readers through these transformative therapeutic approaches, highlighting their potential for healing and self-discovery.

Cognitive Behavioral Therapy (CBT)

Introduction to CBT in Healing Childhood Trauma

Cognitive Behavioral Therapy (CBT) is a well-established therapeutic approach that plays a pivotal role in helping individuals recover from childhood trauma. The core principle of CBT is the interconnectedness of thoughts, feelings, and behaviors. It posits that changing negative thought patterns can lead to positive changes in feelings and behaviors.

Key Components of CBT in Addressing Childhood Trauma

1. Identifying Negative Thought Patterns: CBT aids in recognizing and challenging dysfunctional thoughts that are often rooted in childhood trauma, such as feelings of worthlessness or pervasive fear.

2. Reframing Thoughts: This involves critically examining and challenging the accuracy of negative thoughts, allowing individuals to develop healthier and more realistic ways of thinking.

3. Developing Coping Strategies: CBT provides practical skills to manage distressing emotions and trauma-related symptoms like anxiety, flashbacks, or avoidance behaviors.

4. Empowering the Inner Child: A crucial aspect of CBT in this context is nurturing the wounded inner child by acknowledging their pain, offering compassion, and fostering a sense of safety.

Different Types of CBT and Their Unique Contributions

1. Traditional CBT: Focuses on identifying and changing negative thought patterns and beliefs, effective in treating trauma-related depression and anxiety.

2. Trauma-Focused CBT (TF-CBT): Tailored for children and

adolescents, but also beneficial for adults, it integrates trauma-sensitive interventions with cognitive-behavioral, family, and humanistic principles. Effective in treating PTSD, depression, anxiety, and behavioral issues.

3. Cognitive Processing Therapy (CPT): Effective for PTSD, CPT helps individuals understand and cope with traumatic events by modifying unhelpful beliefs related to trauma.

4. Dialectical Behavior Therapy (DBT): Combines standard CBT techniques with mindfulness, focusing on emotional regulation and distress tolerance. Beneficial for individuals with a history of intense emotional responses due to trauma.

5. Mindfulness-Based Cognitive Therapy (MBCT): Blends CBT methods with mindfulness strategies, effective in preventing depression relapse and aiding trauma survivors in breaking free from negative thought patterns.

6. Acceptance and Commitment Therapy (ACT): Uses acceptance and mindfulness strategies, along with commitment and behavior change techniques, to improve psychological flexibility. Beneficial for a range of issues, including those stemming from childhood trauma.

7. Cognitive Behavioral Analysis System of Psychotherapy (CBASP): Designed for chronic depression, integrating behavioral, cognitive, and interpersonal strategies. Useful for adults who experienced trauma and neglect in early life.

8. Schema Therapy: Combines elements of CBT with other approaches to identify and change deeply rooted patterns established in childhood, leading to recurrent problems in adulthood.

9. Integrative Behavioral Couple Therapy (IBCT): For couples impacted by trauma, focusing on how these experiences affect relationships and teaching ways to improve communication and emotional intimacy.

Each form of CBT offers unique tools and approaches for addressing the specific needs of individuals recovering from childhood trauma. By focusing on altering thought patterns, behaviors, and emotional responses, these therapies provide effective pathways for healing and coping with the lasting effects of traumatic experiences. It's essential for individuals to work with trained therapists to find the most suitable approach for their specific trauma history and recovery goals.

Narrative Therapy

Introduction to Narrative Therapy

Narrative Therapy is a respectful and non-blaming approach to counseling and community work that centers people as the experts in their own lives. Developed by Michael White and David Epston, this therapy views problems as separate from people and assumes that people have many skills, beliefs, values, commitments, and abilities that will assist them in reducing the influence of problems in their lives.

Narrative Therapy's Approach to Childhood Trauma

1. Externalization of Trauma: Narrative Therapy helps individuals externalize their trauma, viewing it as a separate entity from themselves. This technique reduces the identification of an individual with their traumatic experiences, allowing them to rewrite their narrative with more agency and empowerment.

2. Re-Authoring the Story: In Narrative Therapy, a significant emphasis is placed on 're-authoring' one's story. Through this process, individuals who have experienced childhood trauma can reshape their narratives, focusing on resilience and strength rather than victimhood and helplessness.

According to Jill Freedman, a renowned narrative therapist, the approach is particularly effective for childhood trauma as it allows individuals to detach themselves from their experiences and to see their problems as external to their identities.

Narrative Therapy offers a unique and empowering approach to dealing with childhood trauma. By externalizing the problem and re-authorizing the narrative, individuals can gain a new perspective on their experiences, focusing on their strengths and resilience. The evidence from academic journals and case studies, along with expert advice, underlines the effectiveness of Narrative Therapy in providing a path to healing and recovery for those who have experienced childhood trauma. This approach aligns with the contemporary understanding of trauma recovery, emphasizing personal agency and the reclamation of one's story.

GESTALT THERAPY

Gestalt Therapy, with its holistic and experiential approach, offers a unique perspective on treating childhood trauma. This therapy emphasizes the integration of various aspects of an individual's experience, focusing on the present moment while acknowledging the impact of past experiences. Let's dive into the specifics of how Gestalt Therapy approaches childhood trauma.

1. Awareness and the Present Moment

   - Emphasis on "Here and Now": Gestalt Therapy encourages individuals to focus on their current experiences and feelings, rather than getting lost in past events. This focus helps individuals with childhood trauma recognize how these past events are influencing their current thoughts, emotions, and behaviors.

   - Mindfulness and Self-Awareness: The therapy involves techniques that increase mindfulness and self-awareness, helping clients become more aware of their bodily sensations, emotions, and thoughts in the moment.

2. Working with Unfinished Business

   - Resolving Unresolved Issues: Gestalt Therapy identifies and addresses unresolved issues or "unfinished business" from childhood. This might include unexpressed emotions, unmet needs, or unresolved conflicts.

   - Experiential Techniques: Through role-playing and other experiential techniques, individuals can re-enact past situations, confront unresolved feelings, and work through their trauma in a controlled, therapeutic environment.

3. Integration and Acceptance

   - Holistic Integration: The therapy aims to integrate all aspects of an individual's personality. This integration is crucial for individuals who have fragmented aspects of the self due to traumatic childhood experiences.

   - Acceptance of All Experiences: Clients are encouraged

to accept and integrate all their experiences, including traumatic ones, as part of their whole self, leading to greater self-acceptance and healing.

4. Therapeutic Relationship

  ○ Emphasis on Therapist-Client Interaction: Gestalt Therapy places significant importance on the relationship between therapist and client. The therapist acts as a guide to help clients explore their experiences and understand their trauma within the safety of the therapeutic relationship.

5. Creative Experimentation

  ○ Use of Creative and Experiential Methods: Gestalt therapists use a variety of creative and experiential methods to help clients explore and process their traumatic experiences. These may include art, movement, dialogue, and dream work.

Gestalt Therapy's approach to childhood trauma is multifaceted, focusing on awareness, experiential processing, and holistic integration. Its emphasis on the present moment, combined with the therapeutic use of past experiences and the therapeutic relationship, offers a powerful framework for individuals to process and overcome the impacts of their childhood trauma. This approach is supported by various studies and case reports, highlighting its effectiveness in promoting healing and integration for those affected by early traumatic experiences.

ART AND EXPRESSIVE THERAPIES

Art therapy, music therapy, and other expressive therapies offer creative outlets for individuals to explore and express their inner child's emotions. These modalities can be particularly effective for those who find it difficult to articulate their feelings verbally. The *Journal of the American Art Therapy Association* provides numerous examples of how these therapies facilitate emotional expression and healing.

EYE MOVEMENT DESENSITIZATION AND REPROCESSING (EMDR)

EMDR is a therapeutic approach particularly effective for treating trauma. It involves processing distressing memories through a structured approach that includes bilateral stimulation (like eye movements). EMDR helps individuals reprocess traumatic memories, reducing their emotional impact. Research in journals such as the *Journal of EMDR Practice and Research* underscores its success in treating trauma, including childhood trauma.

MINDFULNESS AND MEDITATION

Mindfulness and meditation practices help individuals develop a deeper awareness of their present emotions and thoughts. These practices can be particularly useful in calming the mind and creating a safe space to connect with the inner child. Academic research has shown that mindfulness can reduce symptoms of anxiety and depression, common in those with unresolved childhood trauma.

The therapeutic approaches to healing the inner child are diverse and multifaceted, each offering unique benefits. Whether through psychoanalytic exploration, cognitive restructuring, creative expression, or mindful awareness, these therapies provide pathways to understanding, nurturing, and healing the inner child. Integrating these approaches, often tailored to individual needs and histories, is key to effective healing and long-term emotional well-being.

INNER CHILD WORK EXERCISES

Embarking on inner child work involves engaging in exercises that facilitate the process of connecting with, understanding, and healing the inner child. These exercises are designed to help individuals explore their childhood memories, emotions, and experiences, providing a pathway to healing and personal growth. This subchapter outlines various exercises utilized in inner child work, emphasizing their therapeutic value.

DIALOGUE WITH THE INNER CHILD

One of the most powerful exercises in inner child work is initiating a dialogue with the inner child. This can be done through meditation, where individuals visualize their younger selves and engage in a mental conversation. This dialogue allows for an expression of understanding, compassion, and reassurance to the inner child, addressing feelings of neglect or trauma.

VISUALIZATION TECHNIQUES

Visualization exercises involve creating mental images of protective, nurturing scenarios or revisiting childhood memories with a new perspective. This technique helps in providing a sense of safety and comfort to the inner child, especially in instances where these are lacking.

LETTER WRITING

Writing a letter to one's inner child is a therapeutic exercise that encourages expressing feelings that may have been suppressed or unacknowledged. Similarly, writing a letter from the perspective of the inner child to the adult self can reveal insights into unmet needs and emotions from childhood.

CREATING A SAFE SPACE

Developing a mental or physical 'safe space' is an exercise where individuals create an environment where their inner child feels secure and protected. This space can be visualized in the mind or physically created in a quiet, comforting area in one's home.

SELF-PORTRAIT CREATION

Engaging in art, such as drawing or painting a self-portrait of the inner child, allows for the creative expression of emotions and experiences. This exercise can help in visualizing the inner child and expressing aspects of childhood that may be difficult to articulate in words.

REVISITING CHILDHOOD ACTIVITIES

Participating in activities or hobbies enjoyed during childhood can be a form of reconnecting with the inner child. This exercise helps in recapturing the joy, curiosity, and innocence of childhood, providing a healing experience.

EXPLORING CHILDHOOD PHOTOS

Looking at childhood photographs and reflecting on the feelings and memories they evoke can be a powerful exercise. It allows individuals to reconnect with their past and view their childhood experiences from their adult perspective.

MINDFUL REFLECTION

Mindful reflection involves sitting quietly and allowing childhood memories and emotions to surface without judgment. This practice can help individuals become more aware of the impact of these memories on their current emotional state and behaviors.

Exercises in inner child work are vital tools for healing and personal development. They provide avenues for individuals to explore and reconcile their childhood experiences, leading to emotional healing and a deeper understanding of themselves. Engaging in these exercises, individuals can nurture and validate their inner child, paving the way for a more integrated and emotionally balanced life.

CHALLENGES IN INNER CHILD WORK

COMMON OBSTACLES IN INNER CHILD WORK

Inner child work is a journey that can profoundly impact an individual's path to healing and personal growth. However, this journey is often laden with obstacles that can hinder progress. Recognizing and understanding these common barriers is essential for navigating through them effectively. This subchapter examines the typical obstacles encountered in inner child work and how to address them.

DENIAL OF CHILDHOOD TRAUMA

A significant obstacle in inner child work is the denial or minimization of childhood trauma. Many individuals struggle to acknowledge the full extent of their childhood experiences, often as a coping mechanism. This denial can block the path to healing, as confronting and accepting one's past is crucial for inner child work.

FEAR OF VULNERABILITY

Opening up to the deep-seated emotions and vulnerabilities associated with one's inner child can be daunting. Fear of vulnerability often leads to resistance to fully engaging with the healing process. This fear can stem from a desire to protect oneself from the pain and hurt of past experiences.

Overwhelming Emotions

The intensity of emotions uncovered during inner child work can be overwhelming for some. Feelings of sadness, anger, abandonment, or fear can surface powerfully, sometimes leading to emotional paralysis or distress. Managing these emotions is a crucial part of the healing process.

Lack of Support

Inner child work can be challenging when done in isolation. Lack of support from family, friends, or a therapeutic professional can make the journey feel lonely and insurmountable. Support systems play a vital role in providing encouragement, perspective, and understanding.

Impatience and Unrealistic Expectations

Healing the inner child is not a quick or straightforward process. Impatience and unrealistic expectations about the pace of recovery can lead to frustration and disillusionment. It's important to approach this work with patience and realistic goals.

Difficulty in Breaking Old Patterns

Old habits and coping mechanisms, developed in response to childhood experiences, can be deeply ingrained. Breaking these patterns and adopting new, healthy ways of thinking and behaving can be a significant challenge in inner child work.

Intellectualizing Emotions

Some individuals may find themselves intellectualizing their emotions rather than fully feeling them. This defense mechanism can create a barrier to genuinely connecting with and healing the inner child.

Re-traumatization

In some cases, revisiting childhood traumas can lead to re-traumatization, particularly if not done in a safe and supportive environment. This can set back the healing process and requires careful handling, often with professional guidance.

Understanding and addressing these common obstacles are integral to successful inner child work. Acknowledging the difficulty of facing one's past, embracing vulnerability, managing overwhelming emotions, seeking support, setting realistic expectations, breaking old patterns, genuinely connecting with emotions, and avoiding re-traumatization are all crucial steps in this healing journey. With awareness and the right approach, these obstacles can be navigated, leading to meaningful and transformative healing.

Overcoming Skepticism in Inner Child Work

Inner child work, while a powerful tool in emotional healing and self-discovery, often encounters skepticism. This skepticism can arise from individuals themselves, from others around them, ore ven from a broader cultural perspective that undervalues the impact of childhood experiences on adult life. Overcoming this skepticism is crucial for those embarking on or continuing their journey of inner child work. This subchapter explores ways to address and move beyond skepticism to embrace the transformative potential of inner child work.

Understanding the Roots of Skepticism

Understanding the roots of skepticism in inner child work involves acknowledging the interplay of cultural, personal, and informational factors. In many cultures, there is a prevailing tendency to diminish the impact of emotional experiences, particularly those rooted in childhood. This societal attitude often fosters skepticism about the validity and importance of delving into these early experiences. Additionally, skepticism can emerge as a personal defense mechanism. The process of acknowledging and addressing the needs and wounds of one's inner child can be a painful and challenging endeavor. As a result, some individuals may adopt a stance of skepticism as a means to avoid confronting these uncomfortable emotions. Furthermore, misconceptions about what inner child work actually entails contribute significantly to this skepticism. It's not uncommon for inner child work to be misperceived as overly simplistic or as an unnecessary dwelling on the past. In reality, it is a complex and forward-looking therapeutic process aimed at fostering deep emotional healing and personal growth. Recognizing and understanding these various sources of skepticism is crucial for effectively addressing and overcoming them in the journey of the inner child work.

STRATEGIES TO OVERCOME SKEPTICISM

1. Educating Oneself and Others: Gaining a deeper understanding of what inner child work is and its benefits can help mitigate skepticism.

2. Recognizing the Impact of Childhood Experiences: Acknowledging the profound effect that childhood experiences can have on adult life is a crucial step. Research in developmental psychology and numerous case studies provide evidence of this connection.

3. Starting with Small Steps: For those skeptical about the process, starting with small, manageable steps can help. Engaging in basic self-reflection exercises or journaling can be a less intimidating way to begin exploring one's inner child.

4. Seeking Professional Guidance: Working with a therapist who specializes in inner child work can provide a structured and safe environment to explore this area. Professional guidance can help demystify the process and address specific concerns or doubts.

5. Personal Testimonies and Case Studies: Hearing or reading about the experiences of others who have found inner child work beneficial can be persuasive.

6. Reflecting on Personal Patterns and Behaviors: Self-reflection on one's own life patterns and behaviors can sometimes reveal their roots in childhood experiences. Recognizing these connections can diminish skepticism and open the door to deeper exploration.

7. Patience and Openness: Approaching inner child work with patience and an open mind is crucial. Change and healing take time, and being open to the process, even when septical, can lead to unexpected insights and growth.

Overcoming skepticism in inner child work is often a part of the healing journey itself. By understanding the roots of this skepticism, educating oneself, taking small steps, seeking professional guidance, and staying open to the process, individuals can move beyond doubts to discover the transformative power of reconnecting with and healing their inner child. This journey, while challenging, can lead to profound changes in self-awareness, emotional health, and overall quality of life.

Case-Studies of Inner Child Healing

Inner child work has proven transformative in numerous therapeutic contexts. Here we delve into five detailed case studies that illustrate the healing journey and the profound changes that can occur when individuals engage with their inner child.

Case Study 1: Healing from Parental Neglect

- Background: Jane, a 40-year-old woman, sought therapy for persistent feelings of worthlessness and difficulties in forming close relationships. Her childhood was marked by emotional neglect, with parents who were physically present but emotionally distant.

- Therapeutic Process: Through inner child work, Jane was encouraged to connect with and understand the emotions of her younger self. She engaged in dialogues with her inner child during therapy sessions, providing the comfort and validation she never received from her parents.

- Outcome: This process helped Jane develop self-compassion and recognize her intrinsic worth. Over time, she reported feeling more confident in her relationships and less governed by feelings of inadequacy.

Case Study 2: Resolving Childhood Trauma

- Michael, a 3-year-old, exhibited signs of severe anxiety and social phobia. He had experienced physical and emotional abuse during childhood.

- Therapeutic Process: Michael's therapy included revisiting traumatic childhood memories in a safe space. He used art therapy to express his feelings and began to cultivate a nurturing relationship with his inner child.

- Outcome: Gradually, Michael's anxiety levels decreased. He reported feeling more grounded and was able to form deeper connections with others, something he had struggled with previously.

CASE STUDY 3: ADDRESSING DEEP-ROOTED FEAR OF ABANDONMENT

- Background: Sarah, a 35-year-old, repeatedly found herself in unstable romantic relationships. She had a deep-rooted fear of abandonment stemming from her mother leaving when she was a child.

- Therapeutic Process: In her sessions, Sarah worked on understanding how her fear of abandonment affected her adult relationships. She learned to reassure her inner child of her present-day safety and strength.

- Outcome: Sarah began to choose healthier relationships and developed the ability to be alone without feeling abandoned, significantly improving her emotional well-being.

CASE STUDY 4: CONQUERING CHILDHOOD BULLYING TRAUMA

- Background: Alex, a 28-year-old, faced bullying in school which left him with low self-esteem and trust issues.

- Therapeutic Process: Therapy focused on Alex reconnecting with his inner child and processing the pain and fear caused by the bullying. This included role-playing exercises where adult Alex could offer support to his younger self.

- Outcome: Alex's self-esteem improved, and he reported a decrease in social anxiety. He also found himself more willing to trust others and engage in new social situations.

CASE STUDY 5: OVERCOMING EFFECTS OF EARLY PARENTAL LOSS

- Background: Lisa, a 32-year-old, struggled with persistent sadness and detachment, originating from the loss of her father at a young age.

- Therapeutic Process: Lisa's therapist guided her through a series of reflective exercises where she could express the grief and confusion she felt as a child. She engaged in writing letters to both her younger self and her deceased father.

- Outcome: These exercises allowed Lisa to process her grief more fully. She reported feeling lighter and more connected to her emotions, and her relationships became more meaningful and less guarded.

Each of these case studies offers a glimpse into the transformative power of inner child work. By addressing unresolved childhood issues, individuals were able to overcome deep-rooted emotional challenges and make significant strides in their personal development and emotional health. These success stories stand as a testament to the effectiveness of inner child work in various contexts of emotional healing.

INTEGRATION OF THE INNER CHILD IN ADULT LIFE

The integration of the inner child into adult life is a crucial aspect of the healing journey for those who have experienced childhood trauma. This process involves recognizing, acknowledging, and embracing the inner child's presence and influence in one's daily life Integrating the inner child is not about allowing childish behavior to run rampant; rather, it's about honoring the emotional needs, experiences, and joys that were part of one's childhood. This subchapter explores how to successfully incorporate the inner child into adult existence in a healthy and balanced way.

ACKNOWLEDGING THE INNER CHILD'S PRESENCE

The first step in integration is acknowledging that the inner child exists within the adult self. This means recognizing the ways in which past childhood experiences, both positive and negative, shape current behaviors, reactions, and emotions. By being aware of these influences, adults can start to differentiate between their adult selves and their inner child's responses.

UNDERSTANDING THE INNER CHILD'S NEEDS

Adults must understand the specific needs and wounds of their inner child. This could involve needs for safety, love, validation, or playfulness that were unmet in childhood. Understanding these needs allows adults to address them in healthy ways in their current lives.

Providing Comfort and Reassurance

Once the needs of the inner child are understood, adults can work on providing the comfort and reassurance that the inner child requires. This might involve self-parenting techniques, where the adult learns to offer themselves the love, care, and encouragement that they might not have received as a child.

Balancing the Inner Child's Desires with Adult Responsibilities

Integrating the inner child involves balancing its desires and impulses with the responsibilities and rationality of adult life. This balance allows individuals to experience joy, creativity, and spontaneity while maintaining control and making mature decisions.

Healing Through Play and Creativity

Engaging in activities that foster creativity and play can help adults reconnect with the joy and innocence of their inner child. This might include hobbies, artistic endeavors, or simply incorporating elements of fun and playfulness into everyday life.

Mindfulness and Emotional Regulation

Mindfulness practices can help adults stay aware of when their inner child is influencing their emotional state or behavior. By recognizing these moments, they can choose how to respond in ways that honor their inner child while still acting from their adult self.

Therapeutic Support

Continued therapeutic support can be invaluable in the process of integrating the inner child. Therapy can provide a safe space to explore and understand the inner child's influence and develop strategies for healthy integration.

Integrating the inner child into adult life is a delicate balance that requires awareness, understanding, and a commitment to self-care. By honoring the inner child and addressing its needs, adults can experience a more fulfilling, balanced, and emotionally rich life. This integration is key to not only healing childhood wounds but also embracing a complete and authentic self.

Reparenting Yourself

Understanding Self-Parenting

Heinz Kohut's self-psychology offers a profound framework for understanding the concept of self-parenting, especially in the context of healing and personal growth. This subchapter delves into how Kohut's theories provide a foundation for the concept of self-parenting, focusing on the development and nurturing of the self in the absence of adequate childhood empathy and attunement.

Empathetic Attunement and the Development of the Self

Central to Kohut's self-psychology is the concept of empathetic attunement – the responsive and understanding attention a caregiver provides to a child. This attunement is crucial for the healthy development of the self. In self-parenting, this idea translates to an individuals learning to provide themselves with the empathetic responses they might have missed during their childhood, thus nurturing their own emotional growth.

Mirroring and Idealization Needs

Kohut identified two primary developmental needs in children: mirroring and idealization. In self-parenting, these needs are addressed internally:

- Mirroring: This refers to the validation and positive reinforcement a child receives from caregivers. In self-parenting, mirroring involves recognizing and affirming one's own worth, talents, and successes, essentially providing one with the acknowledgment and encouragement that fosters healthy self-esteem.

- Idealization: This is the child's need to look up to and internalize the qualities of a capable and soothing caregiver. In the context of self-parenting, this involves identifying internal or external sources of strength and stability, which can help in building a secure and resilient self.

COHESIVE SELF AND SELF-DEFICITS

Kohut emphasized the importance of developing a cohesive self. Self-parenting within this framework involves identifying areas of self-deficits – aspects of the self that are underdeveloped due to inadequate empathic responses during formative years. The concept of self-parenting here is to actively work on nurturing and developing these areas to achieve a more integrated and stable sense of self.

TRANSFORMATION OF THE SELF

A key aspect of Kohut's theory is the transformative potential within each individual. Self-parenting is seen as a path to transform and heal the self. This transformation is not just about repairing past wounds but also about evolving and strengthening the self, aligning with one's true potential and aspirations.

Kohut's self-psychology provides a foundational understanding of self-parenting, emphasizing the importance of self-empathy, self-validation, and the nurturing of one's true potential. It offers a pathway for individuals to compensate for the empathetic attunement they lacked during crucial developmental stages, thereby facilitating a journey towards a more integrated, self-compassionate, and robust sense of self.

TECHNIQUES OF SELF-PARENTING

Self-parenting is a therapeutic process of nurturing one's inner child by providing the care, attention, and compassion that may not have been adequately received during childhood. This self-guided journey focuses on healing past wounds and fostering personal growth, Here, we explore various techniques of self-parenting that can help individuals develop a healthier, more nurturing relationship with themselves.

1. Self-Compassion and Kind Self-Talk: One of the fundamental techniques of self-parenting involves cultivating self-compassion. This includes practicing kind and nurturing self-talk, especially in moments of failure or distress. Replace

critical or harsh internal dialogue with words of understanding, encouragement, and love.

2. Mindful Awareness of Inner Child Needs: Develop an awareness of your inner child's needs and emotions. Regularly check in with yourself to understand what you are feeling and why. Acknowledge these feelings without judgment, as a compassionate parent would with their child.

3. Emotional Validation and Expression: Allow yourself to feel and express emotions freely. Whether it's through crying, laughing, or expressing anger in a healthy way, validating and expressing your emotions is key to self-parenting. It's about giving yourself permission to experience and process your feelings.

4. Setting Healthy Boundaries: Just as a good parent sets boundaries for the safety and well-being of their child, self-parenting involves setting healthy boundaries for yourself. Learn to say no, protect your energy, and make decisions that align with your best interests.

5. Meeting Basic Needs: Prioritize meeting your basic needs for rest, nutrition, exercise, and leisure. Ensure that you are taking care of your physical health, as a caring parent would for their child.

6. Engaging in Play and Creativity: Reconnect with your playful and creative side. Engage in activities that you enjoyed as a child or explore new hobbies. This reconnection with playfulness is a vital aspect of nurturing your inner child.

7. Reflective Practices: Engage in reflective practices like journaling or meditation. These practices can help you understand and connect with your inner child, providing insights into your emotional state and unmet childhood needs.

8. Forgiving Yourself and Others: Work on forgiving yourself for past mistakes and forgiving those who may have hurt you in the past. Forgiveness is a powerful tool in healing the inner child and moving forward.

9. Seeking Support: Don't hesitate to seek support from friends, family, or a professional therapist. Sometimes, external guidance and understanding can be invaluable in your self-parenting journey.

10. Celebrating Accomplishments: Acknowledge and celebrate

your achievements, no matter how small. Recognizing your accomplishments is a way of affirming your self-worth and progress.

Self-parenting is a journey of self-discovery and healing. By implementing these techniques, individuals can provide themselves with the love, care, and validation that nurtures their inner child. This process leads to a more fulfilling life, where one can enjoy a deeper sense of inner peace, self-acceptance, and personal resilience.

Choosing Compassion Over Shame

In the realm of emotional healing and personal growth, the shift from shame to compassion is a crucial transition. Shame, a deeply ingrained emotion often rooted in early negative experiences, can significantly hinder personal development and well-being. This subchapter explores how individuals can replace feelings of shame with self-compassion, drawing on academic research, case studies, and expert opinions.

Understanding the Nature of Shame

Shame is the emotion that involves feeling deeply flawed and unworthy of love or belonging. It is distinct from guilt, which is about feeling bad about one's actions. According to Brene Brown, a renowned researcher in the field of shame and vulnerability, shame can lead to self-destructive behaviors and a significant decline in mental health. It often originates from early life experiences, such as criticism, neglect, or abuse.

The Role of Self-Compassion

Self-compassion, as posited by Dr. Kristin Neff, is a healthier alternative to shame. It involves being kind to oneself in the face of failures or mistakes, understanding one's experiences as part of the shared human experience, and holding one's feelings in mindful awareness. Self-compassion has been shown in numerous studies to promote resilience, well-being, and a more positive outlook on life.

Techniques for Shifting from Shame to Compassion

1. Mindfulness and Emotional Awareness: The first step in

overcoming shame is to become aware of its presence without judgment. Mindfulness practices help in recognizing and accepting feelings of shame.

2. Reframing the Internal Dialogue: Changing how one speaks to oneself is crucial. This involves challenging the negative self-talk that fuels shame and replacing it with a more compassionate, understanding inner voice.

3. Understanding the Universality of Suffering: Recognizing that suffering and imperfection are part of the human experience helps diminish the isolation that shame often brings.

4. Self-Forgiveness: Letting go of past mistakes and understanding that everyone errs can help in alleviating shame. Self-forgiveness is a key step in embracing self-compassion.

5. Connecting with Others: Sharing one's feelings and experiences with trusted individuals can help alleviate the sense of isolation that comes with shame. Social support is vital in fostering a sense of belonging and acceptance.

6. Cultivating Self-Empathy: Developing empathy towards oneself, as one would towards a friend in distress, is an effective way to combat shame. This can involve nurturing activities, self-care, and speaking kindly to oneself.

EMPIRICAL EVIDENCE SUPPORTING THE TRANSITION

Research has consistently shown the benefits of self-compassion over shame. Studies published in journals such as *The Journal of Personality and Social Psychology* and *Psychological Science* have documented how self-compassion leads to greater emotional resilience, reduced anxiety and depression, and improved mental health.

Replacing shame with compassion is a transformative process that significantly enhances emotional well-being and personal growth. The journey involves mindfulness, reframing internal dialogue, understanding common humanity, practicing self-forgiveness, seeking social support, and cultivating self-empathy. This shift not only diminishes the painful effects of shame but also opens the door to a more fulfilling, resilient, and compassionate life.

LONG-TERM BENEFITS

The process of healing the inner child, while often challenging, yields significant long-term benefits that extend beyond mere emotional relief. This healing journey not only addresses past wounds but also facilitates profound personal transformation and growth. Drawing from psychological research and therapeutic insights, this subchapter will explore the enduring advantages that arise from the healing of the inner child.

1. Enhanced Emotional Well-Being: One of the most immediate benefits of healing the inner child is an overall improvement in emotional well-being. Individuals often experience a significant decrease in anxiety, depression, and emotional distress. This improvement is a direct result of addressing and resolving deep-seated emotional wounds from childhood.

2. Improved Relationships: Healing the inner child can lead to healthier and more fulfilling relationships. By understanding and healing past traumas, individuals often find themselves better equipped to form secure attachments, communicate more effectively, and set healthy boundaries. This transformation can lead to more meaningful connections with others.

3. Increased Self-Esteem and Confidence: Addressing the issues of the inner child often results in a notable increase in self-esteem and self-confidence. As individuals reconcile with their past and begin to understand and accept themselves more fully, they typically experience a greater sense of self-worth.

4. Greater Self-Awareness: The journey of healing the inner child fosters a deep level of self-awareness. Individuals become more attuned to their needs, desires, and emotional triggers. This awareness is crucial for making conscious, healthy life choices and for navigating future challenges with greater understanding and resilience.

5. Reduction in Self-Sabotaging Behaviors: Many self-sabotaging behaviors stem from unresolved childhood issues. Healing the inner child can help individuals recognize and change these behaviors, leading to healthier coping mechanisms and life choices.

6. Development of Healthy Copings Strategies: The process of healing the inner child equips individuals with effective coping strategies for dealing with stress and adversity. These strategies are often more adaptive and constructive compared to those

developed in response to childhood trauma.

7. Reconnection with Joy and Playfulness: Healing the inner child can rekindle a sense of joy, creativity, and playfulness. Rediscovering these aspects can enrich one's life experience, contributing to overall happiness and fulfillment.

8. Breaking Cycles of Trauma: For those who have experienced intergenerational trauma, healing the inner child can be an essential step in breaking these cycles. This healing not only benefits the individual but can also positively impact future generations.

9. Improved Physical Health: There is a well-documented connection between emotional health and physical well-being. Healing the inner child can lead to improvements in physical health, as emotional stress and trauma can have direct phsyical manifestations.

The long-term benefits of healing the inner child are comprehensive, touching every aspect of an individual's life. This healing journey, while rooted in addressing past wounds, opens the door to a life marked by emotional health, fulfilling relationships, personal growth, and a reconnection with the most authentic parts of oneself. It is a path not just to recovery but to transformation and profound personal development.

CONCLUSION

As we conclude this chapter on healing the inner child, it's important to recognize that this journey is one of profound courage and resilience. The path to reconnecting with and nurturing your inner child is not always easy, but it is immensely rewarding. It invites a deeper understanding of oneself, fosters emotional healing, and opens the door to a more authentic and fulfilling life.

Throughout this chapter, we have explored various therapeutic approaches, practical exercises, and the common challenges that arise in the process of inner child work. We've seen how each approach offers unique insights and tools for healing. From the depths of psychoanalytic exploration to the transformative power of narrative therapy, each modality provides a pathway to understanding and nurturing the wounded child within.

The case studies and success stories shared in this chapter are testaments to the resilience of the human spirit and the transformative power of inner child work. They serve as reminders that healing is possible, no matter the depth of one's wounds. These stories underscore the value of patience, perseverance, and self-compassion on this healing journey.

As you move forward, remember that healing your inner child is a process that unfolds over time. It requires patience, self-compassion, and a willingness to embrace vulnerability. The journey may bring to light deeply buried emotions and memories, but it also brings the opportunity for profound personal growth and emotional freedom.

The long-term benefits of this work are immeasurable. By healing your inner child, you open yourself to a life marked by greater emotional well-being, healthier relationships, and a deeper sense of self-acceptance. This journey allows you to live more fully in the present, free from the constraints of past traumas and unmet childhood needs.

In closing, honor your inner child as an integral part of who you are. Embrace the journey of healing with an open heart and mind. The path may be challenging, but it is also filled with opportunities for growth, discovery, and transformation. your inner child holds the key to unlocking a more authentic, joyful, and fulfilling life. Cherish and nurture this part of yourself, and step forward into a future of healing and hope.

CHAPTER SUMMARY

- Embracing Non-linearity in Healing: The journey to heal the inner child is inherently non-linear, requiring patience and understanding as one navigates through emotional ups and downs.

- Diverse Therapeutic Techniques: A range of therapeutic approaches, including psychoanalytic, cognitive-behavioral, and narrative therapies, play a crucial role in addressing the intricate needs of the inner child.

- Transformative Power of Inner Child Work: Engaging in inner child work leads to profound emotional healing, improved relationships, and increased self-esteem.

- Overcoming Common Challenges: Recognizing and addressing challenges such as denial of childhood trauma, fear of vulnerability, and overwhelming emotions are integral to successful inner child work.

- Moving Beyond Skepticism: Educating oneself about the benefits and processes of inner child work helps in overcoming skepticism and embracing its transformative potential.

- Long-Term Benefits of Healing: The journey offers long-lasting benefits including enhanced emotional well-being, better relationships, and a deeper connection with oneself.

- Integration of the Inner Child: Successfully incorporating the inner child into adult life involves balancing its needs with adult responsibilities, leading to a richer emotional experience.

- Self-Parenting Techniques: Techniques like self-compassion, mindful awareness, and emotional validation are key in nurturing and healing the inner child.

- Shift from Shame to Compassion: Replacing feelings of shame with self-compassion through mindfulness and reframing internal dialogues contributes to emotional healing and personal growth.

APPLY IT!

Journal Prompts

1. Reflecting on Healing Progress: What are the most significant changes you've noticed in yourself since beginning your inner child work? How have these changes affected your daily life and relationships?

2. Challenges and Triumphs: What have been the biggest obstacles in your journey of healing the inner child? How have you managed to overcome these challenges, and what have you learned from them?

3. Revisiting Past Experiences: Choose a specific event from your childhood that had a significant impact. How do you view this

event now from your adult perspective? What insights can you gain from re-examining this experience?

4. Envisioning the Future: How do you see your journey of inner child work influencing your future? What hopes or aspirations do you have for your ongoing healing and growth?

Suggested Goals

1. Developing Self-Compassion: Practice daily self-compassion by replacing one negative self-statement with a positive affirmation each day, tracking progress in a journal, and reviewing changes bi-weekly.

2. Exploring Creative Expression: Dedicate one hour each week to a chosen creative activity, such as painting, writing, or playing music, creating at least one piece of work per week, and setting aside a specific time for this over the next six months.

3. Healing Through Play: Engage in a playful activity weekly, like a childhood hobby or a new game, and commit to this practice for three months, with a weekly check-in to reconnect with the joy and spontaneity of your inner child.

4. Self-Parenting Strategies: Implement a daily self-parenting ritual, like morning affirmations or evening gratitude reflections, practicing these rituals daily and evaluating the emotional impact monthly.

5. Forgiveness and Acceptance: Work on forgiving one past incident or person each week through activities like writing forgiveness letters or meditative practices, documenting feelings in a journal, and reviewing the emotional impact every two weeks

6. Complete the exercises in Chapter 7 of the *Childhood Trauma and Recovery Workbook* to deepen your understanding and apply the concepts discussed.

8

What Are Other Healing Techniques?

EMBRACING HOLISTIC APPROACHES FOR DEEPER HEALING

"The soul always knows what to do to heal itself. The challenge is to silence the mind." – Caroline Myss

Embarking on a healing journey from childhood trauma involves exploring a multitude of avenues, beyond the realms of traditional psychotherapy. This chapter unfolds a tapestry of alternative healing techniques, each offering a unique perspective and method to address the deep-seated effects of early trauma. From the grounding practices of mindfulness and meditation to the expressive liberation found in art and movement therapies, we venture into holistic approaches that engage the body, mind, and spirit.

Recognizing the intricate connection between physical well-being and emotional health, this chapter emphasizes the role of physical activities, such as yoga and tai chi, in trauma recovery. These practices not only foster bodily awareness and control but also contribute to emotional regulation and stress reduction. The chapter further explores the these practices not only foster bodily awareness and control but also contribute to emotional regulation and stress reduction. The chapter further explores the therapeutic benefits of creative expression, whether through art, writing, music, or dance, highlighting how these mediums can unlock emotional insights and foster a sense of empowerment and self-discovery.

Understanding that healing extends to one's lifestyle and dietary choices, the chapter delves into the impact of nutrition on mental health. It discusses how a balanced diet, mindful eating, and the avoidance of certain substances can significantly influence one's emotional state and stress levels. Additionally, we consider the importance of creating a supportive and nurturing environment, emphasizing the role of community, relationships, and self-care routines in the holistic recovery process.

Mind Body Practice

Understanding Mind-Body Connection in Trauma Recovery

Trauma recovery transcends the conventional boundaries between the mind and the body, as contemporary research emphasizes the significance of the mind-body connection in the healing process. This concept underscores the understanding that psychological trauma often manifests physically, leading to symptoms like tension, headaches, and fatigue, thereby highlighting the direct impact of psychological distress on the body. Simultaneously, trauma can alter brain structures involved in stress response, emotion regulation, and memory, which can significantly influence physical health and stress levels.

Recognizing the mind-body connection in trauma recovery involves incorporating physical approaches into psychological healing. Techniques such as yoga, mindfulness, and breathwork play a crucial role in regulating the body's stress response and improving emotional balance. Among the most influential contributors to this field is Dr. Bessel van der Kolk, whose work, particularly in *The Body Keeps the Score*, compiles extensive research and clinical experience. He explains how traumatic experiences alter brain functioning and contribute to physical health issues. His advocacy for an integrated approach to trauma treatment, which includes both psychotherapeutic and somatic methods, has been pivotal in shaping modern strategies for trauma recovery.

In conclusion, understanding the mind-body connection is essential in trauma recovery. This holistic approach, which treats trauma as an experience affecting both mind and body, encourages the use of body-based therapies alongside traditional psychological methods. This integrative approach, highlighted by Dr. Bessel van der Kolk's research, opens the door for more effective and comprehensive trauma treatments, acknowledging the intertwined nature of mental and physical health in the aftermath of traumatic experiences.

YOGA AND TRAUMA

Yoga, an ancient practice that integrates physical postures, breath control, and meditation, has emerged as a significant therapeutic tool in trauma recovery. The effectiveness of yoga in this context is not just anecdotal but is increasingly supported by scientific research. It offers a unique approach to healing, focusing on the mind-body connection that is crucial in addressing the aftermath of trauma.

YOGA'S ROLE IN ADDRESSING TRAUMA

1. Physical and Psychological Benefits: Yoga facilitates a connection with the body, which is often disrupted in individuals who have experienced trauma. The practice encourages mindfulness, body awareness, and relaxation, which are vital in managing stress and trauma-related symptoms.

2. Restoring Autonomy and Control: Trauma can lead to feelings of helplessness and a loss of control over one's body. Yoga empowers individuals by giving them control over their movements and breathing, helping to restore a sense of autonomy and self-efficacy.

YOGA'S THERAPEUTIC PRACTICES IN TRAUMA RECOVERY

1. Trauma-Sensitive Yoga: This specialized form of yoga is tailored to meet the needs of trauma survivors. It emphasizes creating a safe, non-judgmental space where individuals can explore body sensations and develop a mindful connection with their physical selves.

2. Breathing Techniques: Controlled breathing is a key component of yoga that helps regulate the body's stress response. These techniques can be particularly beneficial for trauma survivors in managing anxiety and emotional dysregulation.

EXPERT INSIGHTS

In his influential work, Dr. Bessel van der Kolk, a leading trauma expert, underscores the therapeutic value of yoga in trauma recovery. His research, published in the *Journal of Clinical Psychiatry*, demonstrates yoga's effectiveness in reducing PTSD symptoms, particularly hyperarousal, a common challenge for trauma survivors. Dr. van der Kolk advocates for integrating yoga into trauma therapy, highlighting its ability to combine physical postures and mindful breathing to recalibrate the nervous system. This approach not only decreases PTSD symptoms but also fosters a more harmonious relationship between individuals and their bodies, addressing the dysregulation often caused by trauma.

Yoga offers a powerful and accessible tool for individuals recovering from trauma. By fostering mind-body awareness, reducing symptoms of hyperarousal, and restoring a sense of bodily autonomy, yoga can play a crucial role in the healing process.

MINDFULNESS AND MEDITATION

Mindfulness and meditation have become pivotal in modern psychotherapy for trauma recovery, drawing significantly from the teachings of the late spiritual teacher Thich Nhat Hanh. His approach to mindfulness, emphasizing living mindfully and peacefully in the present, has proven beneficial for trauma survivors, particularly through practices like mindful breathing and walking. These techniques focus on enhancing present-moment awareness, crucial for those troubled by past traumas or future anxieties, and regulating emotional responses, thereby lessening the intensity of reactions triggered by traumatic memories. Clinical research in psychology supports the effectiveness of these practices, especially in improving PTSD symptoms by helping individuals detach from traumatic memories and reduce trauma-linked arousal. Mindfulness-Based Stress Reduction (MBSR), developed by Dr. Jon Kabat-Zinn, is one such adaptation that uses mindfulness to assist trauma survivors in managing stress and emotional discomfort. Thich Nhat Hanh's legacy in mindfulness continues to influence trauma therapy, underscoring the value of these practices in fostering healing, and offering a path to resilience and well-being for those impacted by trauma.

TAI CHI AND QIGONG

Tai Chi and Qigong, with their roots in ancient Chinese practices, offer significant therapeutic benefits in recovering from childhood trauma. These practices focus on slow, deliberate movements and coordinated breath control, enhancing body awareness and regulation – key aspects often disrupted by traumatic experiences. They are particularly effective in reducing stress and anxiety, common symptoms in individuals who have experienced childhood trauma. Research, including studies published in the *Journal of Alternative and Complementary Medicine*, has highlighted their effectiveness in improving psychological well-being, emphasizing their role in reducing stress and enhancing emotional balance. Integrating Tai Chi and Qigong into holistic healing programs for trauma survivors complements traditional therapies, aiding in the physical component of emotional and psychological healing. By fostering the mind-body connection, these practices help re-establish the crucial link between physical sensations and emotional states, thereby facilitating comprehensive healing for those affected by early traumatic experiences.

BREATHWORK IN TRAUMA THERAPY

Breathwork, an effective therapeutic technique involving controlled and mindful breathing, is increasingly recognized for its role in trauma therapy. It employs various breathing methods to regulate the body's stress response, crucial for individuals healing from trauma. Notably, a study by Dr. Richard Brown and Dr. Patricia Gerbarg in *The Healing Power of the Breath* highlights the profound impact of breathwork on reducing trauma-related symptoms like anxiety and hyperarousal. By consciously altering breathing patterns, breathwork aids in calming the nervous system and facilitating emotional regulation. This approach is particularly valuable in trauma therapy as it offers individuals a practical tool to manage distressing emotions and bodily sensations triggered by traumatic experiences. The incorporation of breathwork into trauma recovery strategies emphasizes its effectiveness in not just addressing psychological aspects of trauma but also its physical manifestations, providing a comprehensive path towards healing and resilience.

UNDERSTANDING AND BALANCING CHAKRAS

The concept of chakras, originating from ancient Indian philosophy, refers to various focal points used in a variety of meditation practices. The chakras are conceived as an energy system that, when balanced, can contribute significantly to overall well-being and healing, including recovery from trauma.

ROLE OF CHAKRAS IN TRAUMA RECOVERY

Each chakra is associated with different aspects of emotional and psychological well-being. Trauma can cause imbalances in these energy centers, leading to emotional and psychological disturbances. Here are the main chakras and their locations

1. Root Chakra (Muladhara): Located at the base of the spine, in the tailbone area. It's associated with feelings of security, stability, and basic needs.

2. Sacral Chakra (Svadhisthana): Positioned about two inches below the navel and two inches inwards. This chakra relates to our sexuality, creativity, and emotional well-being.

3. Solar Plexus Shakra (Manipura): Found in the upper abdomen in the stomach area. It's linked to our ability to be confident and in control of our lives.

4. Heart Chakra (Anahata): Located at the center of the chest, just above the heart. This chakra represents our ability to love and be compassionate.

5. Throat Chakra (Vishuddha): Found in the throat region. It governs our ability to communicate verbally.

6. Third Eye Chakra (Ajna): Situated on the forehead, between the eyebrows. It's the center of intuition and foresight.

7. Crown Chakra (Sahasrara): Located at the very top of the head. This chakra represents our ability to be fully connected spiritually.

Balancing these chakras is believed to promote overall well-being, especially crucial in trauma recovery. Traumatic experiences can disrupt the energy balance of these chakras, leading to emotional and psychological disturbances. Holistic therapy experts like Anodea Judith, author of *Wheels of Life: A User's Guide to the Chakra System*, emphasize the importance of chakra balancing through practices such as meditation, yoga, and energy healing. These chakra-focused practices, when integrated with other therapeutic methods like yoga and mindfulness, provide a comprehensive approach to healing. This holistic integration addresses the interplay of emotional, psychological, and physical aspects of trauma, offering a pathway toward emotional balance, healing, and well-being for those affected by trauma.

NUTRITION

THE GUT-BRAIN CONNECTION

In recent years, the scientific community has significantly advanced our understanding of the gut-brain connection and its pivotal role in overall health, particularly in relation to childhood trauma. This subchapter explores how nutrition influences this connection, impacting the healing process from childhood trauma.

THE GUT-BRAIN AXIS: A BIDIRECTIONAL PATHWAY

The gut-brain axis is a complex, bidirectional communication system linking the enteric nervous system of the gastrointestinal tract with the central nervous system. According to a study in the *Journal of Clinical Gastroenterology*, this connection not only regulates digestive functions but also influences emotional cognitive centers in the brain.

IMPACT OF CHILDHOOD TRAUMA ON THE GUT-BRAIN CONNECTION

Childhood trauma can disrupt this delicate balance, leading to a range of physiological and psychological issues. A study in *Psychoneuroendocrinology* highlights how traumatic stress can alter gut microbiota, potentially leading to gastrointestinal disorders and exacerbating mental health conditions like anxiety and depression.

NUTRITIONAL INTERVENTIONS FOR HEALING

Recognizing the influence of diet on the gut-brain axis opens new avenues for healing from childhood trauma.

    1. Probiotics and Gut Health: The inclusion of probiotics in the diet is widely recognized for its beneficial effects on gut health.

There is a growing body of research suggesting that balancing gut microbiota through probiotics can be helpful in managing symptoms of anxiety and depression, particularly those that might be exacerbated by trauma.

2. Anti-Inflammatory Foods: Inflammation is a common aftermath of chronic stress. Consuming anti-inflammatory foods, such as omega-3 fatty acids found in fish and flaxseed, as suggested in *Brain, Behavior, and Immunity*, can mitigate this response.

3. Balancing Blood Sugar Levels: Fluctuations in blood sugar can impact mood and energy levels. A balanced diet rich in whole grains, lean proteins, and vegetables can stabilize these levels, enhancing emotional regulation.

4. Dietary Diversity for Mental Health: Diverse diets provide a range of nutrients crucial for brain health. A study in *BMC Medicine* links diet diversity to lower rates of depression and anxiety.

5. Avoiding Processed Foods: There is a growing understanding that consuming highly processed foods may contribute to increased inflammation and disrupt gut microbiota. This dietary pattern is often linked with a higher risk of mood disorders, such as depression.

Addressing the nutritional needs of individuals who have experienced childhood trauma is crucial in the healing process. By focusing on a diet that supports gut health and reduces inflammation, it's possible to positively influence the gut-brain connection, paving the way for both physical and emotional healing. This approach, backed by growing scientific evidence, underscores the importance of a holistic perspective in addressing the complex aftermath of childhood trauma.

NUTRITIONAL STRATEGIES FOR STRESS REDUCTION

Nutritional strategies play a significant role in managing and reducing stress, particularly for individuals recovering from childhood trauma. A well-balanced diet can substantially impact one's mental health and stress levels. This subchapter delves into how specific dietary approaches can aid in alleviating stress and promoting emotional well-being.

THE ROLE OF NUTRITION IN STRESS MANAGEMENT

The connection between diet and stress response is well-documented in scientific research. As per a study in *Nutrients*, certain foods can modulate the body's physiological response to stress, influencing neurotransmitter production and hormonal balance, which is essential for managing stress levels.

KEY NUTRITIONAL STRATEGIES FOR STRESS REDUCTION

1. Incorporating Magnesium-Rich Foods: Magnesium plays a crucial role in stress response regulation. Foods like leafy greens, nuts, and seeds can enhance the body's resilience to stress.

2. Boosting Omega-3 Fatty Acid Intake: Omega-3 fatty acids, particularly EPA and DHA found in fish oil, have been shown to reduce the effects of stress and anxiety.

3. Complex Carbohydrates for Serotonin Production: Complex carbohydrates, such as those found in whole grains, are widely understood to play a role in the production of serotonin, a neurotransmitter associated with feelings of calmness. Influcing complex carbs in the diet is generally considered beneficial for enhancing modo and helping to manage stress.

4. Antioxidant-Rich Foods for Oxidative Stress: Foods rich in antioxidants, such as berries and dark chocolate, combat oxidative stress. This is particularly relevant for individuals with a history of trauma, where oxidative stress is often elevated.

5. Herbal Supplements and Teas: natural supplements like green tea, which contains theanine, and adaptogens like ashwagandha, have been found to be effective in stress reduction.

6. Adequate Protein Intake: Protein-rich foods contribute to neurotransmitter synthesis and energy levels, helping in stress management.

7. Limiting Caffeine and Sugar: Reducing the intake of caffeine and high-sugar foods can prevent the spikes and crashes in energy and mood that exacerbate stress.

A strategic approach to nutrition can be a powerful tool in reducing stress and aiding in the recovery from childhood trauma. By focusing on a diet that supports brain health, balances neurotransmitters, and stabilizes energy levels, individuals can significantly mitigate the impact of stress on their mental and physical health. These nutritional strategies, backed by scientific research, offer a practical and accessible means of enhancing the resilience and well-being of those on a journey of recovery from childhood trauma.

ADDRESSING INFLAMMATION AND PHYSICAL HEALTH POST-TRAUMA

The aftermath of childhood trauma often extends beyond psychological effects, manifesting in physical health issues, particularly chronic inflammation. This subchapter explores the link between childhood trauma and inflammation and outlines strategies to address and mitigate these physical health concerns.

THE LINK BETWEEN CHILDHOOD TRAUMA AND INFLAMMATION

Childhood trauma has been identified as a significant factor in the development of chronic inflammation in later life. A study published in *Brain, Behavior, and Immunity* highlights the correlation between adverse childhood experiences and elevated levels of pro-inflammatory cytokines. This chronic inflammation can lead to various health issues, including autoimmune diseases, cardiovascular disorders, and metabolic syndromes.

STRATEGIES TO ADDRESS INFLAMMATION POST-TRAUMA

1. Anti-Inflammatory Diet: Adopting a diet rich in anti-inflammatory foods is a critical step. Foods high in omega-3 fatty acids (like salmon and flaxseeds), antioxidants (found in berries and leafy greens), and fiber (from whole gains and legumes) are known to reduce inflammation.

2. Exercise: Exercise has been shown to lower inflammatory markers. Activities like brisk walking, swimming, or yoga can be particularly beneficial.

3. Stress Management Techniques: Since stress can exacerbate inflammation, employing stress reduction techniques like mindfulness meditation, deep breathing exercises, and

progressive muscle relaxation is essential.

4. Adequate Sleep: Quality sleep is crucial in regulating the body's inflammatory responses.

5. Avoidance of Pro-Inflammatory Substances. Reducing the intake of processed foods, sugars, and trans fats, which can trigger inflammation, is recommended. Additionally, it's widely advised to limit alcohol consumption and to quit smoking, as these habits are also associated with increased inflammation and other health risk s.

6. Regular Health Check-Ups: Regular medical check-ups to monitor inflammatory markers and overall health can help in the early detection and management of any inflammation-related conditions.

Recognizing and addressing inflammation and its associated physical health issues is a crucial aspect of holistic recovery from childhood trauma. By integrating an anti-inflammatory lifestyle, encompassing diet, exercise, stress management, and sleep hygiene, individuals can significantly improve their physical health and overall well-being post-trauma. These strategies, supported by academic research and clinical studies, offer practical approaches to mitigate the long-term physical effects of early life trauma, paving the way for a healthier, more balanced life.

Supplements and Herbs in Trauma Recovery

The role of supplements and herbs in the context of healing from childhood trauma is an area that has garnered increasing interest in recent years. This subchapter explores how certain supplements and herbal remedies can support the recovery process by alleviating some of the physiological and psychological symptoms associated with trauma.

The Role of Supplements and herbs in Healing

Nutritional and herbal supplements can play a supportive role in trauma recovery. They are often used to address specific symptoms like anxiety, depression, sleep disturbances, and the physical manifestations of stress, which are commonly experienced by trauma survivors.

Key Supplements and Herbs for Trauma Recovery

1. Omega-3 Fatty Acids: Omega-3 supplements, found in fish A study in the oil, have been shown to reduce symptoms of depression and anxiety. A study in the *Journal of Clinical Psychiatry* highlights their potential in mood regulation.

2. Magnesium: Magnesium is known for its calming effects on the nervous system. It can aid in reducing anxiety and improving sleep quality.

3. B-Vitamins: B-Vitamins, particularly B6, B9 (folate), and B12, have been linked to better mental health. They play a crucial role in brain chemistry and neurotransmitter function.

4. Vitamin D: Often dubbed the 'sunshine vitamin,' Vitamin D deficiency has been linked to increased susceptibility to stress and depression.

5. Adaptogenic Herbs: Herbs like Ashwagandha, Rhodiola, and Holy Basil are known as adaptogens. They help the body resist stressors and have been shown to reduce cortisol levels, improving stress response and overall well-being.

6. CBD Oil: Cannabidiol (CBD) has gained attention for its potential in managing anxiety and PTSD symptoms.

7. Valerian Root and Chamomile: These herbs are often used for their sedative properties, aiding in sleep and relaxation.

Supplements and herbs can be valuable tools in the journey of healing from childhood trauma. By supporting the body's physiological response to stress and aiding in emotional regulation, these natural remedies can enhance overall well-being. However, it's imperative to approach their use with care and guidance from healthcare professionals, and as part of a comprehensive treatment plan. This integrative approach, backed by scientific research, can significantly contribute to a more effective and holistic recovery process.

CREATING A BALANCED TRAUMA RECOVERY DIET

Nutrition plays a pivotal role in the journey of healing from childhood trauma. A balanced trauma recovery diet can profoundly impact both physical and mental health, aiding in the regulation of mood, energy levels, and overall well-being. This subchapter explores the components of such a diet, emphasizing the importance of specific nutrients and diety patterns in trauma recovery.

The Importance of Nutrition in Trauma Recovery

The connection between diet and mental health is increasingly recognized in the field of psychonutrition. Nutrition psychiatry research suggests that what we eat significantly affects our brain function, and, consequently, our emotional and psychological well-being.

Key Elements of a Trauma Recovery Diet

1. Whole Foods: Focus on whole, unprocessed foods that are rich in nutrients. These include fruits, vegetables, whole grains, lean proteins, and healthy fats. Whole foods provide essential vitamins, minerals, and antioxidants that support brain health and stress resilience.

2. Omega-3 Fatty Acids: Omega-3 fatty acids, commonly found in fatty fish, flaxseeds, and walnuts, are important for brain health. There is a general consensus in nutritional science that omega-3s are beneficial, and their inclusion in the diet has been associated with a positive impact on mood and potentially a reduced risk of depression.

3. Complex Carbohydrates: Carbohydrates from whole grains, legumes, and vegetables provide steady energy and help in the production of serotonin, a neurotransmitter that enhances mood and reduces stress.

4. Lean Proteins: Adequate protein intake is vital for neurotransmitter function. Sources include lean meat, fish, eggs, dairy, legumes, and nuts.

5. Fermented Foods: Fermented foods like yogurt, kefir, sauerkraut, and kimchi contain probiotics, which can positively influence gut health and, by extension, mental health.

6. Hydration: Adequate hydration is crucial for cognitive function and overall health. Water, herbal teas, and hydrating foods like cucumbers and melons are good choices.

7. Moderation of Caffeine and Sugar: High consumption of caffeine and sugar can exacerbate anxiety and lead to mood swings. Moderation is key.

A balanced trauma recovery diet is a fundamental component of healing from childhood trauma. By incorporating nutrient-rich foods, focusing on whole and unprocessed items, and maintaining a balanced approach, individuals can significantly support their mental and physical recovery process. This dietary approach, combined with other therapeutic methods and professional guidance, can pave the way for a healthier, more resilient life post-trauma.

CREATIVE EXPRESSION

ART THERAPY IN TRAUMA RECOVERY

Art therapy, a form of expressive therapy that uses the creative process of making art to improve physical, mental, and emotional well-being, has emerged as a significant modality in addressing childhood trauma. This subchapter explores how art therapy facilitates trauma recovery, offering a unique and powerful channel for expression and healing.

THE ROLE OF ART THERAPY IN CHILDHOOD TRAUMA RECOVERY

1. Non-Verbal Expression: For any survivors of childhood trauma, verbalizing feelings can be challenging. Art therapy provides a non-verbal medium to express complex emotions and experiences that might be hard to articulate.

2. Processing Traumatic Memories: Art can help externalize and contain traumatic memories, making them more manageable. It allows individuals to safely explore and process traumatic events from their past.

3. Enhancing Self-Awareness and Insight: Engaging in art-making can lead to increased self-awareness and insights into one's inner world and traumatic experiences, fostering a deeper understanding of oneself.

TECHNIQUES AND APPROACHES IN ART THERAPY FOR TRAUMA

1. Drawing and Painting: Allows for the expression of emotions and traumatic memories through visual forms, colors, and symbols.

2. Sculpture and Clay Work: Useful in expressing and managing intense emotions, helping to rebuild a sense of control and resilience.

3. Collage Making: Enables the combination of various images and materials to create a narrative, which can be particularly therapeutic in processing complex trauma.

4. Mask-Making: This can be used to explore different aspects of identity and the impact of trauma on one's sense of self.

THE THERAPEUTIC BENEFITS OF ART THERAPY

- Empowerment: Art therapy empowers individuals by providing a sense of control over the artistic process and, by extension, over their trauma narrative.

- Stress Reduction: Engaging in creative activities has been shown to reduce stress and promote relaxation.

- Improved Communication Skills: Art therapy can enhance communication skills, helping individuals articulate their thoughts and feelings more effectively.

- Building Emotional Resilience: The process of creating art and reflecting on the created pieces can build emotional resilience and coping skills.

Art therapy offers a transformative path for individuals recovering from childhood trauma. It provides a unique way to express, process, and heal from traumatic experiences, without the need for words. By facilitating emotional release, self-discovery, and personal growth, art therapy can be a vital component in the journey toward healing and wholeness. This creative therapeutic approach, supported by a nurturing and understanding environment, can significantly contribute to long-term recovery and emotional well-being.

WRITING AND JOURNALING

Writing and journaling are powerful therapeutic tools in the journey of healing from childhood trauma. This subchapter explores the role of these self-expressive practices in processing traumatic experiences, aiding in emotional release, and fostering personal growth.

The Therapeutic Power of Writing and Journaling

1. Facilitating Emotional Expression: Writing provides a safe and private outlet for expressing feelings and thoughts associated with traumatic experiences, often difficult to verbalize.

2. Processing Traumatic Memories: Journaling can help in organizing and making sense of confusing and painful memories, allowing for a deeper understanding and integration of these experiences.

3. Enhancing Self-Reflection: Regular writing encourages introspection, helping individuals to reflect on their internal states, understand their reactions to trauma, and recognize patterns in their behavior and thoughts.

Techniques in Writing and Journaling for Trauma Recovery

1. Free Writing: Encourages writing without inhibition about one's feelings and thoughts, which can be particularly cathartic for releasing bottled-up emotions related to trauma.

2. Structured Journaling: Involves writing responses to specific prompts or questions that target aspects of the trauma or its impact on current life.

3. Letter Writing: writing unsent letters to different figures (e.g., abusers, caregivers, or even oneself) can provide a means to express unspoken feelings and thoughts.

4. Narrative Writing: Involves creating a coherent narrative of the traumatic experiences, which can help in gaining perspective and reducing the distress associated with fragmented memories.

Benefits of Writing and Journaling in Trauma Therapy

- Reduction of Stress and Anxiety: Writing about traumatic events has been shown to reduce stress and anxiety, improving overall mental health.

- Cognitive Processing: Helps in organizing thoughts, making sense of traumatic experiences, and integrating them into one's life story.

- Empowerment and Control: Gives a sense of control over one's story, helping to shift from a victim mindset to a tone of empowerment and resilience.

- Enhancing Coping Skills: Regular journaling can improve coping strategies and emotional regulation, essential in the aftermath of trauma.

Writing and journaling offer accessible and potent means of navigating the complex path of healing from childhood trauma. They provide a voice to the unspoken, a structure to the chaotic, and a narrative to the fragmented experiences of trauma. Engaging in these practices can significantly aid in the journey toward understanding, acceptance, and emotional healing, contributing to long-term resilience and well-being.

MUSIC AND SOUND THERAPY

Music and sound therapy have merged as effective therapeutic tools in addressing the complex layers of childhood trauma. This subchapter delves into the role of music and sound in facilitating emotional expression, cognitive processing, and overall healing in individuals who have experienced trauma during childhood.

THE HEALING PROPERTIES OF MUSIC AND SOUND THERAPY

1. Emotional Resonance: Music's ability to evoke and modulate emotions makes it a powerful medium for expressing and processing feelings associated with childhood trauma

2. Neurological Impact: Research indicates that music can positively influence brain areas affected by trauma, such as the amygdala and hippocampus, aiding in emotional regulation (Hanna-Pladdy & Mackay, 2001).

3. Creating a Safe Space: Soundscapes or certain musical compositions can create a feeling of safety and comfort, essential for individuals dealing with trauma-related anxiety and stress.

TECHNIQUES IN MUSIC AND SOUND THERAPY FOR TRAUMA RECOVERY

1. Active Music Making: Involves engaging in creating music, such as playing instruments or singing, which can be empowering and cathartic for trauma survivors.

2. Music Listening and Analysis: listening to specific pieces of music and discussing their emotional impact can help individuals explore and articulate their feelings related to traumatic experiences.

3. Sound Healing: Utilizing instruments like Tibetan singing bowls, tuning forks, or gongs, sound healing sessions can promote relaxation and emotional release.

4. Vocal Expression: Encourages using one's voice in singing or chanting, which can be particularly powerful in reclaiming one's voice and sense of self, often stifled by childhood trauma.

BENEFITS OF MUSIC AND SOUND THERAPY IN TRAUMA RECOVERY

- Stress Reduction: engaging with music can lower cortisol levels, reducing the overall stress response, which is often heightened in trauma survivors.

- Enhanced Emotional Expression: Provides a non-verbal outlet for expressing and processing complex emotions tied to traumatic events.

- Improved Cognitive Processing: Music therapy can aid in the reorganization of traumatic memories, facilitating better cognitive processing and integration.

- Increased Mindfulness and Presence: Focused listening and musical engagement can enhance mindfulness, helping individuals remain grounded in the present moment.

Music and sound therapy offer unique and profound pathways for healing from childhood trauma. By engaging with music and sound, individuals can explore and process their traumatic experiences in a supportive and non-threatening environment. These therapeutic modalities not only facilitate emotional expression and cognitive processing but also contribute to a deeper sense of connection with oneself and others, playing a vital role in the journey toward healing and wholeness.

DANCE AND MOVEMENT THERAPY

Dance and Movement Therapy (DMT) is an expressive therapy form that uses body movement as a means of communication and expression. Its application in the context of childhood trauma recovery is gaining recognition due to its holistic approach to healing, encompassing the physical, emotional, and psychological aspects of a person.

THE THERAPEUTIC ROLE OF DANCE AND MOVEMENT

1. Body Awareness and Expression: DMT fosters a deeper connection with the body, helping individuals become more aware of their physical sensations and expressions. This awareness is vital for those who have experienced trauma in their early years, as trauma often leads to disconnection from the body (Koch, et al).

2. Processing Trauma Physically: Trauma is stored in the body and can manifest as physical symptoms. DMT provides a safe way to release this stored trauma through movement, aiding in the healing process.

3. Empowerment and Control: Childhood trauma can leave individuals feeling powerless. Dance and movement empower them by providing control over their bodies and movements, restoring a sense of agency.

TECHNIQUES IN DANCE AND MOVEMENT THERAPY FOR TRAUMA RECOVERY

1. Structured and Freeform Movement: Therapy may include structured dances or freeform movement, allowing individuals to explore and express their emotions and experiences through their bodies.

2. Rhythmic Coordination: Engaging in rhythmic activities can be soothing and regulating for the nervous system, especially beneficial for those with trauma-related anxiety or PTSD.

3. Mirroring Exercises: Involves therapists mirroring a client's movements, which can foster empathy, validation, and

connection.

4. Body Mapping: A process where individuals use movement to explore and communicate their trauma stories, mapping them onto their physical selves.

BENEFITS OF DANCE AND MOVEMENT THERAPY IN TRAUMA RECOVERY

- Improved Emotional Regulation: Regular engagement in DMT can lead to better management of emotions, a common challenge for those who have experienced childhood trauma.

- Enhanced Self-Esteem: As individuals gain control and mastery over their movements, they often experience an increase in self-esteem and confidence.

- Decreased Symptoms of Depression and Anxiety: The physical activity involved in DMT can reduce symptoms of depression and anxiety, often comorbid with trauma.

- Strengthened Mind-Body Connection: Helps in reconciling and integrating the body as a safe and expressive part of oneself, essential for those who have experienced trauma.

Dance and Movement Therapy offers a dynamic and potent avenue for healing from childhood trauma. It allows individuals to reconnect with their bodies, express unspeakable emotions, and reclaim a sense of empowerment lost in traumatic experiences. As a holistic therapeutic approach, DMT addresses the complexities of trauma recovery, making it an invaluable tool in the journey toward healing and wholeness.

INTEGRATING CREATIVE PRACTICES INTO DAILY LIFE

Integrating creative practices into daily life is a vital strategy for individuals recovering from childhood trauma. Creative activities such as art, writing, music, and dance offer therapeutic benefits, helping to process complex emotions and experiences that are often difficult to articulate verbally. This subchapter explores practical ways to weave these practices into everyday routines for ongoing healing and self-expression.

THE VALUE OF CREATIVE PRACTICES IN HEALING

1. Expression Beyond Words: Creative activities allow for the expression of feelings that might be too deep or painful for words, facilitating a deeper understanding and processing of trauma.

2. Regulation of Emotions: Engaging in creative practices can have a calming effect, helping regulate emotions by focusing the mind and soothing the nervous system.

3. Building Self-Esteem and Identity: Creative endeavors can enhance self-esteem and help in rebuilding a sense of identity, often fragmented by traumatic childhood experiences.

INCORPORATING CREATIVITY INTO DAILY LIFE

1. Art Journaling: Keeping an art journal can be a daily practice where one can draw, paint, or collage feelings and thoughts, serving as a visual diary of the healing journey.

2. Writing Rituals: Setting aside time each day for reflective writing, such as journaling or poetry, can be a powerful tool for introspection and processing emotions.

3. Music and Mindfulness: Incorporating music into daily routines, whether it's listening, singing, or playing an instrument, can be a therapeutic way to engage with emotions and memories.

4. Movement and Dance: Integrating simple movement or dance into daily routines, even for a few minutes, can help maintain a connection with the body and release pent-up emotions.

5. Photography as Reflection: Taking photographs can be a form of mindfulness and a way to see the world through a different lens, helping to find beauty and meaning in the everyday.

MAKING CREATIVE PRACTICES ACCESSIBLE

- Start Small: Begin with small, manageable creative activities that don't feel overwhelming. Even a few minutes a day can be beneficial.

- Create a Dedicated Space: If possible, designate a small area in your home as a creative space, encouraging regular engagement in creative activities.

- Combine Creativity with Routine: Integrate creative practices with daily routines, like drawing while listening to a podcast or writing during morning coffee.

Overcoming Barriers to Creativity

- Addressing Perfectionism: Encourage a mindset of exploration and expression rather than perfection or mastery in creative activities.

- Dealing with Emotions/intensity: Sometimes, creative expression can bring intense emotions to the surface. It's important to practice self-care and seek support when needed.

- Finding What Resonates: Experiment with different forms of creativity to find what feels most therapeutic and fulfilling.

Incorporating creative practices into daily life offers a powerful, accessible way for individuals recovering from childhood trauma to process their experiences, express emotions, and rebuild a sense of self. These practices, woven into the fabric of everyday life, can become a cornerstone of ongoing healing and personal growth, contributing significantly to the journey toward wholeness and resilience.

Sleep

Understanding the Relationships Between Trauma and Sleep

Sleep disturbances are a common and significant consequence of traumatic experiences, particularly those stemming from childhood. The intricate relationship between trauma and sleep is multifaceted, affecting both the quality and pattern of sleep. Studies in the field of psychotraumatology provide valuable insights into how traumatic experiences disrupt normal sleep architecture and physiology.

How Trauma Affects Sleep

1. Disruption of Normal Sleep Patterns: Traumatic experiences, especially in childhood, can alter the brain's neurochemistry and hormonal balance, leading to disrupted sleep patterns. This disruption can manifest as difficulties in falling asleep, staying asleep, or experiencing restorative sleep. According to research

in the *Journal of Clinical Sleep Medicine*, trauma can significantly impact the rapid eye movement (REM) and non-REM sleep stages, crucial for emotional regulation and memory processing.

2. Hyperarousal and Hypervigilance: One of the hallmarks of Post-Traumatic Stress Disorder (PTSD) is a state of hyperarousal, where the individual remains on high alert for perceived threats. This heightened state of anxiety and vigilance can make it challenging to relax and fall asleep. As per a study in the *European Journal of Psychotraumatology*, this hyperarousal is linked to changes in the brain's fear-response systems, which remain activated even during sleep, leading to disturbed sleep.

3. Trauma-Related Nightmares: Recurrent nightmares and night terrors are common among those who have experienced trauma, particularly in childhood. These nightmares often involve reliving the traumatic event and can be so distressing that individuals may avoid sleep or experience severe anxiety around bedtime. A study in the *American Journal of Psychiatry* notes that trauma-related nightmares are not just mere reflections of the traumatic event but also a manifestation of unresolved emotional conflict.

4. The Role of the Brain's Sleep Centers: Trauma can affect the brain areas responsible for regulating sleep, such as the hypothalamus and the pineal gland, which are involved in the production of melatonin, a hormone that regulates sleep-wake cycles. Alterations in these areas can lead to long-term changes in sleep patterns.

5. Emotional Distress and Sleep: The emotional distress that stems from trauma, encompassing feelings like sadness, anger, or guilt, can also disrupt sleep. This emotional turmoil can hinder achieving a relaxed state conducive to good sleep quality.

6. Trauma's Physical Impact on Sleep: Physical symptoms related to trauma, such as chronic pain or gastrointestinal issues, can further exacerbate sleep problems.

Understanding the relationships between trauma and sleep is crucial for comprehending the full impact of traumatic experiences, especially those from childhood. This complex interplay underscores the need for a holistic approach to addressing the sleep disturbances that often accompany trauma. Addressing these sleep issues is not only essential for improving sleep quality but also for the overall healing process from trauma.

THERAPEUTIC APPROACHES TO TRAUMA-RELATED SLEEP ISSUES

Dealing with trauma-related sleep issues is a critical aspect of recovery from childhood trauma. Sleep disturbances, such as insomnia, nightmares, and broken sleep patterns, are common in individuals who have experienced trauma during childhood. This subchapter looks into the various therapeutic approaches that can help address and alleviate these sleep issues, enhancing the overall healing process.

COGNITIVE BEHAVIORAL THERAPY FOR INSOMNIA (CBT-I)

Cognitive Behavioral Therapy for insomnia is a highly effective treatment for insomnia, particularly in individuals with a history of trauma. CBT-I focuses on changing sleep habits and the mindset about sleep.

Key Components:

- Sleep Restriction Therapy: Restricting the time spent in bed to consolidate sleep and increase sleep efficiency.

- Stimulus Control Instructions: Developing a consistent sleep schedule and using the bed only for sleep and intimacy.

- Addressing negative beliefs and fears about sleep that stem from traumatic experiences.

Studies in the *Journal of Clinical Sleep Medicine* have shown that CBT-I significantly improves sleep quality and reduces the symptoms of insomnia in trauma survivors.

EYE MOVEMENT DESENSITIZATION AND REPROCESSING (EMDR)

EMDR is a well-established therapy for trauma processing, which can indirectly improve sleep by addressing the root cause of the trauma. It involves recalling distressing events while receiving bilateral sensory input, such as side-to-side eye movements, which helps in processing and integrating traumatic memories. By resolving the underlying trauma, EMDR can reduce nightmares and night terrors, common in individuals with PTSD, as reported in the *Journal of EMDR Practice and Research*.

MINDFULNESS-BASED STRESS REDUCTION (MBSR)

MBSR is a program that incorporates mindfulness meditation to reduce stress and improve emotional regulation, thereby aiding in better sleep. It includes practices like body scan meditation, sitting meditation, and mindful yoga. MBSR helps calm the mind and reduces the hyperarousal associated with trauma, leading to improved sleep patterns.

TRAUMA-INFORMED YOGA

Trauma-informed yoga is tailored to the needs of trauma survivors, focusing on creating a safe space for individuals to reconnect with their bodies. Practicing yoga encourages a sense of safety and presence in the body and helps regulate the nervous system and can be particularly soothing before bedtime.

BIOFEEDBACK AND NEUROFEEDBACK

These therapies use monitoring devices to provide feedback on physiological functions, empowering individuals to gain control over their body's responses. It focuses on controlling the heart rate, muscle tension, and breathing, which can be disrupted by trauma. It targets brainwave patterns associated with relaxation and calmness. As per the *Journal of Applied Psychophysiology and Biofeedback*, these therapies can improve sleep quality by enhancing self-regulation skills.

LIFESTYLE CHANGES TO SUPPORT BETTER SLEEP

Lifestyle changes can play a significant role in enhancing sleep quality and overall well-being. This subchapter explores practical lifestyle adjustments that can support better sleep for individuals healing from childhood trauma.

ESTABLISHING A CONSISTENT SLEEP ROUTINE

- Set Fixed Sleep and Wake Times: Even on weekends, try to go to bed and wake up at the same time each day.

- Establish a Pre-Sleep Ritual: Engage in calming activities like reading or taking a warm bath before bed.

CREATING A SLEEP-INDUCING ENVIRONMENT

- Comfortable Bedding: Invest in a comfortable mattress and pillows.

- Control Light Exposure: Use blackout curtains or a sleep mask to block out light

- Maintain a Cool Temperature: The ideal bedroom temperature for sleep is around 64 degrees Fahrenheit.

INCORPORATING CREATIVITY INTO DAILY LIFE

1. Art Journaling: Keeping an art journal can be a daily practice where one can draw, paint, or collage feelings and thoughts, serving as a visual diary of the healing journey.

2. Writing Rituals: Setting aside time each day for reflective writing, such as journaling or poetry, can be a powerful tool for introspection and processing emotions.

3. Music and Mindfulness: Incorporating music into daily routines, whether it's listening, singing, or playing an instrument, can be a therapeutic way to engage with emotions and memories.

4. Movement and Dance: Integrating simple movement or dance into daily routines, even for a few minutes, can help maintain a connection with the body and release pent-up emotions.

5. Photography as Reflection: Taking photographs can be a form of mindfulness and a way to see the world through a different lens, helping to find beauty and meaning in the everyday.

PHYSICAL ACTIVITY AND EXERCISE

- Engage in Regular Exercise: Preferably in the morning or afternoon

- Avoid Intense Workouts Close to Bedtime: They can increase alertness and make it difficult to fall asleep.

STRESS REDUCTION AND RELAXATION TECHNIQUES

- Mindfulness Meditation: Helps in calming the mind and

preparing for sleep.

- Deep Breathing Exercises: useful for relaxation before bedtime.

- Progressive Muscle Relaxation: A method to relax the body by tensing and relaxing muscles.

Managing Screen Time

- Limit Screen Time Before Bed: Avoid phones, tablets, and computers at least an hour before bedtime.

- Use Blue Light Filters: On devices in the evening if necessary.

Incorporating these lifestyle changes can significantly enhance the quality of sleep for individuals recovering from childhood trauma. It's important to remember that these adjustments may require time to show results and be tailored to each individual's preferences and needs. Consistency and patience are key in making these changes effective parts of a trauma recovery routine, leading to better sleep and overall improved health and well-being.

Physical Health

Managing Chronic Pain and Physical Symptoms

Managing chronic pain and physical symptoms resulting from childhood trauma involves a multifaceted approach. research indicates that childhood trauma, particularly emotional abuse, significantly predicts pain catastrophizing, a mental state wherein individuals perceive their pain as worse than it actually is. This remains significant even when controlling for depression and anxiety Effective strategies to manage these symptoms include:

1. Mindfulness-Based Stress Reduction (MBSR): Techniques like meditation and yoga can help manage stress and reduce the intensity of physical symptoms.

2. Cognitive-Behavioral Therapy (CBT): Helps in changing the perception of pain and developing coping strategies.

3. Physical Therapy and Exercise: Regular physical activity and guided therapy can improve pain management and overall

physical health.

4. Somatic Experiencing: Focuses on resolving the physical sensations associated with traumatic memories.

5. Medical Interventions: In some cases, medication or other treatments may be necessary to manage chronic pain.

6. Integrative Medicine: Combining traditional medicine with alternative therapies for a holistic approach.

7. Diet and Nutrition: A balanced diet can improve overall health and help mitigate physical symptoms.

8. Building a Support Network: Engaging with support groups or therapy provides emotional support, crucial in dealing with chronic pain and physical symptoms.

These strategies aim to address both the psychological and physical aspects of trauma, emphasizing a comprehensive approach to healing.

THE ROLE OF EXERCISE IN PHYSICAL HEALING

The role of exercise in physical healing from childhood trauma is profound. It's not just about physical well-being, but also mental and emotional recovery. Regular physical activity, as noted in studies like those in *The Journal of Clinical Psychiatry*, helps mitigate symptoms of PTSD and depression, which are common in those with a history of childhood trauma. Exercise triggers the release of endorphins, natural mood lifters, promoting stress relief and emotional well-being. Dr. Bessel van der Kolk, a trauma expert, advocates for exercise in treatment plans, emphasizing its role in re-establishing a connection with the body. This connection is vital for those healing from trauma. Tailored to individual needs and preferences, exercise becomes a therapeutic tool, enhancing self—esteem and providing a sense of accomplishment. It also improves sleep quality, crucial for both physical and emotional healing. In summary, exercise is a key component in the holistic approach to recovering from childhood trauma, addressing physical, emotional, and psychological aspects of well-being.

DEVELOPING A SELF-CARE ROUTINE FOR PHYSICAL HEALTH

Creating a self-care routine focused on physical health is a vital step in healing from childhood trauma. It involves a holistic approach that integrates various elements essential for physical and emotional well-being.

1. Regular Exercise: Include activities like yoga, walking, or swimming that you enjoy. Tailor your exercise routine to fit your preferences, ensuring it brings joy and not stress.

2. Nutritious Diet: Focus on a balanced diet rich in fruits, vegetables, lean proteins, and whole grains. Pay attention to how different foods affect your mood and energy levels.

3. Adequate Sleep: Establish a regular sleep schedule. Create a calming bedtime routine to enhance sleep quality, crucial for healing.

4. Mindfulness Practices: Incorporate mindfulness or meditation into your routine to stay connected with your body and the present moment, aiding in stress reduction.

5. Hydration and Supplements: Stay well-hydrated and consider supplements or vitamins, as recommended by a healthcare provider, to support your body's needs.

6. Regular Medical Check-Ups: schedule regular check-ups and screenings. Address any chronic physical issues with your healthcare provider.

7. Self-Compassion: Remember to be kind to yourself. Recognize your efforts and progress, no matter how small.

8. Social Interaction: Engage in social activities that uplift your spirits and provide a sense of community and support.

9. Relaxation Techniques: Incorporate relaxation practices like deep breathing, aromatherapy, or warm baths to reduce stress and promote physical relaxation.

10. Limit Unhealthy Habits: Reduce or eliminate habits like smoking, excessive alcohol consumption, or unhealthy eating patterns.

Remember, your self-care routine should be flexible and adaptable to your changing needs and circumstances. It's about finding what works best for you and consistently incorporating these practices into your daily life for overall health and recovery.

Exploring Dreams

Dream exploration is a crucial component of childhood trauma recovery offering profound insights into the subconscious mind. Dreams often act as reflections of unresolved emotions and memories related to traumatic experiences. Psychoanalytic theories, particularly those of Freud and Jung, view dreams as key to unlocking repressed feelings and thoughts. In therapy, dream analysis is used to interpret symbols and narratives that emerge in dreams, shedding light on the individual's inner conflicts and trauma.

Modern psychological research further supports the therapeutic value of dream exploration in trauma recovery. Studies suggest that dreams play a vital role in emotional processing, especially in integrating traumatic memories. This is reflected in therapeutic practices where dream interpretation forms a part of the healing process. Through techniques such as dream journaling and discussing dreams with a therapist, individuals can gain a deeper understanding of how their childhood trauma influences their current mental and emotional state.

Dream exploration can reveal the profound impact of past experiences on present-day behaviors and emotions. It facilitates a journey into the subconscious, offering a pathway to uncover and heal deep-seated trauma. Engaging with dreams allows for a transformative process, where hidden aspects of the self are revealed and integrated, leading to a more holistic recovery.

In summary, dream exploration in childhood trauma recovery is a powerful tool for understanding and resolving subconscious trauma. It leverages psychoanalytic principles and modern research, providing a unique window into the depths of the psyche and facilitating emotional healing and integration.

Building Emotional Intelligence

Emotional Intelligence (EI), a concept popularized by psychologist Daniel Goleman, encompasses the ability to recognize, understand, and manage one's own emotions, as well as to recognize and influence the emotions of others. Goleman's work, delineated in his book *Emotional Intelligence*, highlights EI as a key factor in personal success and mental health. In the context of childhood trauma recovery, understanding and developing EI is crucial, as traumatic experiences often distort emotional perception and regulation. Studies in journals like the *American Journal of Psychiatry* have shown a link between low EI and trauma-related disorders like PTSD. EI involves four key skills:

1. Self-Awareness: Cultivate an understanding of your emotions. Practices like mindfulness and journaling can help you identify and acknowledge your feelings.

2. Self-Management: Work on regulating your emotions. Techniques like deep breathing, meditation, and physical exercise can be effective in managing emotional responses.

3. Social Awareness: Improve empathy and understanding of others' emotions. This can involve active listening and trying to perceive situations from others' perspectives.

4. Relationships Management: Develop skills to interact positively with others. This includes clear communication, conflict resolution, and being open to feedback.

These skills collectively facilitate better-coping mechanisms, healthy relationships, and improved overall well-being. For trauma survivors, enhancing EI can lead to more effective processing of traumatic memories and emotions, reducing the long-term impact of trauma. Experts like Dr. Bessel van der Kolk, in his book *The Body Keeps the Score*, emphasize the role of EI in recognizing and addressing the somatic symptoms of trauma. By developing EI, Individuals can better navigate their emotional landscape, leading to a more balanced and fulfilling life post-trauma.

CONCLUSION

As we conclude this exploration into the diverse world of healing techniques for childhood trauma, it's evident that the path to recovery is as varied and unique as the experiences that shape us. This journey is not just about overcoming trauma but also about rediscovering oneself and finding new sources of strength and resilience. The techniques discussed in this chapter, from mindfulness and creative expression to nutritional adjustments and innovative therapies, underscore the importance of a holistic approach to healing. They offer hope and varied paths for individuals seeking to heal the wounds of their past.

The key takeaway is that healing from childhood trauma is not a linear process but a journey that encompasses mind, body, and spirit. It requires patience, compassion, and the courage to explore various therapeutic avenues. As we navigate through these diverse methodologies, we find that each one offers unique insights and tools for healing. By embracing these varied approaches, individuals can tailor their recovery journey to their specific needs, preferences, and experiences.

In the end, healing from childhood trauma is about more than just alleviating pain; it's about building a life of meaning, joy, and fulfillment. The techniques and strategies outlined in this chapter are not just pathways to recovery; they are stepping stones to a transformed life, one where the shadows of the past no longer cloud the potential of the present and future. As we close this chapter, let it be a reminder that each step taken in this journey is a step towards a brighter, more empowered se lf.

CHAPTER SUMMARY

- Holistic Healing Approaches: Exploring a variety of healing techniques, beyond traditional psychotherapy, can offer unique perspectives and methods to address childhood trauma.

- Mind-Body Practices: Activities like yoga and tai chi not only enhance physical well-being but also contribute to emotional regulation and stress reduction, crucial in trauma recovery.

- Creative Expression: Art, music, writing, and dance are powerful mediums for unlocking emotional insights and fostering self-discovery and empowerment.

- Nutrition and Mental Health: A balanced diet and mindful eating significantly influence emotional states and stress levels, highlighting the importance of nutrition in trauma recovery.

- Supportive Environments: Creating nurturing environments and fostering positive relationships are essential for holistic recovery and emotional healing. erupted by childhood understanding Trauma and Sleep: Traumatic experiences, particularly in childhood, can significantly disrupt normal sleep patterns and physiology, leading to challenges like insomnia, hyperarousal, and trauma-related nightmares.

- Exercise and Physical Healing: Engaging in regular, moderate exercises such as yoga, swimming, or walking helps alleviate chronic pain and improves physiological responses disrupted by childhood trauma, thereby enhancing overall physical healing.

- Developing Emotional Intelligence: Enhancing emotional intelligence is key to processing traumatic memories and emotions, reducing the long-term impact of trauma.

APPLY IT!

Journal Prompts

1. Exploring Alternative Therapies: Reflect on any alternative or holistic therapies you've tried or are interested in for healing from childhood trauma. What draws you to these methods?

2. Nutrition and Mood: Journal about the connection between your diet and emotional well-being. Have you noticed changes in your mood or stress level with certain foods?

3. Creative Expression: Describe how engaging in a creative activity (like art, music, or writing) has helped you process your emotions related to childhood trauma.

4. Physical Activity and Healing: Reflect on how physical activities, like yoga or exercise, have impacted your trauma recovery. What changes have you noticed?

Suggested Goals

1. Try a New Healing Technique: Over the next month, experiment with a new therapy or healing technique (like Tai Chi, Qigong, or art therapy) and note any changes in your emotional state.

2. Nutritional Adjustment for Mood Improvement: Commit to adjusting one aspect of your diet for a month to see how it affects your mood and stress levels. This could involve increasing your intake of fruits and vegetables, reducing processed foods, or adding probiotics.

3. Regular Creative Activity: Set a goal to engage in a creative

activity, like journaling or painting, at least twice a week for the next month to express and explore your emotions.

4. Consistent Exercise Routine: Aim to incorporate a form of physical exercise, such as walking or yoga, into your daily routine for the next six weeks, observing its impact on your physical and emotional health.

5. Complete the exercises in Chapter 8 of the *Childhood Trauma and Recovery Workbook* to deepen your understanding and apply the concepts discussed.

Conclusion

EMBRACING RESILIENCE: A JOURNEY BEYOND CHILDHOOD TRAUMA

"Healing doesn't mean the damage never existed. It means the damage no longer controls our lives."- Akshay Dubey

As we conclude this journey, it's essential to embrace the courage and resilience inherent in healing your inner child. This path, though strewn with challenges, illuminates the extraordinary potential for recovery and personal growth. Healing the inner child is a transformative process, offering deeper self-understanding, emotional healing, and the promise of a more authentic and fulfilling life.

Our exploration of various therapeutic approaches and practical exercises has provided valuable tools for addressing past traumas. Each modality has opened pathways to understanding and nurturing the inner child, aiding in emotional healing and growth.

Remember, healing is a gradual process, demanding patience, self-compassion, and vulnerability. This journey uncovers buried emotions and memories, yet also offers a chance for profound personal growth and emotion liberation. The benefits of this healing journey are boundless, leading to enhanced emotional well-being, healthier relationships, and a deeper sense of self-acceptance. It empowers you to live more fully in the present, unshackled from the past's constraints.

In this healing journey, we also discover the hidden strengths forged by past traumas. Survivors often develop remarkable resilience, empathy, and self-awareness. Many become advocates or leaders, using their experiences to effect positive change. A creative expression often flourishes, offering unique perspectives and solutions. This journey instills a sense of strength, courage, and appreciation for life's joys, leading to significant personal growth and transformation.

In closing, honor and embrace your inner child as a core part of your being. Approach this healing path with an open heart and mind, ready for growth, discovery, and transformation. Your inner child is the key to unlocking a more authentic, joyful, and fulfilling existence. Cherish and nurture this part of yourself as you step forward into a future filled with healing, hope, and the positive potential that emerges from overcoming childhood trauma. You are equipped for this journey. You've got this!

Chapter Summary

- Transformation Through Healing: Healing the inner child is a transformative journey, leading to a deeper understanding of oneself, emotional recovery, and a more genuine life.

- Patience and Self-Compassion: Healing is gradual, requiring patience, self-compassion, and the courage to face buried emotions and memories for profound personal growth.

- Empowerment and Present Living: This journey empowers one to live fully in the present, free from the constraints of past traumas, enhancing emotional well-being and self-acceptance.

- Resilience and Strength from Trauma: Trauma survivors often develop resilience, empathy, and self-awareness, using their experiences for advocacy and creative expression.

- Celebrating the Inner Child: Embrace and honor your inner child as a fundamental part of your identity, paving the way for a future filled with healing, hope, and new possibilities.

APPLY IT!

Journal Prompt

1. Reflect on your journey of healing the inner child. How have you grown and what strengths have you discovered in yourself? How do you envision using these insights to shape your future?

Suggested Goals

1. Applying Book Learnings In Daily Life: Make a commitment to apply the key insights and strategies you've learned from the book in your everyday life. This could involve setting aside time each day for practices highlighted in the book, such as engaging in a brief mindfulness exercise, journaling to connect with your inner child, or utilizing specific coping techniques during challenging moments. The goal is to incorporate these learnings into your daily routine, continuously nurturing your emotional well-being and solidifying the resilience you've developed throughout your healing journey.

2. Childhood Trauma and Recovery: Healing Your Inner Child Workbook Companion: Consider purchasing Childhood Trauma and Recovery: Healing Your Inner Child Workbook Companion to enrich your healing journey. Aim to engage with it regularly, completing exercises or reflections at least once a week. This companion serves as a structured tool to deepen your insights, track your progress, and practically apply the concepts learned in our journey of healing the inner child.

3. Complete the exercises in the Conclusion section of the *Childhood Trauma and Recovery Workbook* to deepen your understanding and apply the concepts discussed.

Appendix

Appendix A: Works Cited
Appendix B: Feelings Wheel
Appendix C: Childhood Trauma Assessment Checklist
Appendix D: Comprehensive Healing Progress Tracker
Appendix E: What's Next?

Works Cited

"2023 Science of Tai Chi & Qigong as Whole-Person Health Conference Abstract Supplement." Journal of Integrative and Complementary Medicine, vol. 29, supp. 2, 2023, pp. A-28-A-A-48, Mary Ann Liebert Inc., doi: 10.1089/jicm.2023.29125.abstracts.

Albrahim, Tarfa, et al. "Effects of Regular Exercise and Intermittent Fasting on Neurotransmitters, Inflammation, Oxidative Stress, and Brain-Derived Neurotrophic Factor in Cortex of Ovariectomized Rats." *Nutrients*, vol. 15, no. 4270, 2023.

American Art Therapy Association. "What is Art Therapy? Fact Sheet." American Art Therapy Association, 2022, www.arttherapy.org/what-is-art-therapy. Accessed 12 Jan. 2024.

American Psychiatric Association. "Definition of Trauma." *American Psychiatric Association*, 2013, www.psychiatry.org.

American Psychological Association. *American Psychological Association.* www.apa.org. Accessed 12 Jan. 2024.

Baisas, Laura. "PTSD Patients' Brains Work Differently When Recalling Traumatic Experiences." *Yale University News*, 30 Nov, 2023.

Bowlby, John and Mary Ainsworth. "Attachment Theory: The Formation of Human Relationships." *Developmental Psychology*, vol. 28, 1992, pp. 759-775.

Bradshaw, John. Homecoming: *Reclaiming and Healing Your Inner Child.* Bantam, 1990.

Bremner, J.D. "Trauma and the Amygdala: Hyperactivity and Enlargement." *Neuropsychopharmacology*, 2024.

Brown, Brene. *The Gifts of Imperfection: Let Go of Who You Think You're Suppose to Be and Embrace Who You Are.* Hazelden Publishing, 2010.

Brown, Richard P., and Patricia L. Gerbarg. *The Healing Power of the Breath*. 1st ed., Shambhala, 2012.

Centers for Disease Control and Prevention and Kaiser Permanente. "The Adverse Childhood Experiences (ACE) Study." Centers for Disease Control and Prevention, 2024, www.cdc.gov/violenceprevention/aces/index.html.

Child Welfare Information Gateway. "Neglect as a Form of Maltreatment." *Child Welfare Information Gateway*, U.S. Department of Health and Human Services, 2019, www.childwelfare.gov.

Engel-Yeger, Batya, Dafna Palgy-Levin, and Rachel Lev-Wiesel. "The Sensory Profile of People with Post-Traumatic Stress Symptoms." Occupational Therapy in Mental Health, vol. 29, no. 3, 2013, pp. 266-278. doi: 10.1080/0164212.

Feemster, John C., et al. "Trauma-Associated Sleep Disorder: A Posttraumatic Stress/REM Sleep Behavior Disorder Mash-Up? *Journal of Clinical Sleep Medicine*, vol. 15, no. 2, 2019.

Fuchs, Thomas, and Sabine C. Koch. Embodied Affectivity: On Moving and Being Moved." *Frontiers in Psychology*, vol. 5, 2014, p. 91840, doi:10.3389/fpsyg.2014.00508. Accessed 13 Jan. 2024.

Gershuny, Beth S., and Julian F. Thayer. "Relations among Psychological Trauma, Dissociative Phenomena, and Trauma-related Distress: A Review and Integration." *Clinical Psychology Review*, vol. 19, no. 5, 1999, pp. 631-657, doi:10/1016/S0272-7358(98)00103-2. Accessed 12 Jan 2 024.

Goleman, Daniel. *Emotional Intelligence*. 10th Anniversary ed., Bantam, 2005.

Hamilton, Nancy A., et al. "Cognitive Behavioral Therapy for Insomnia Treatment Attrition in Patients with Weekly Nightmares." *Journal of*

Clinical Sleep Medicine, vol. 10, no. 11, 2023, doi: 10.5664/jcsm.10710.

Hanh, Thich Nhat. *The Miracle of Mindfulness: An Introduction to the Practice of Meditation.* Beacon Press, 1975.

Hanna-Pladdy, Brenda, and Alicia MacKay. "The Relation Between Instrumental Musical Activity and Cognitive Aging." *Neuropsychology,* vol. 25, no. 3, 2011, pp. 378-386. PubMed, doi:10.1037/a0021895

Harris, Nadine Burke, et al. *Center for Youth Wellness.* www.centerforyouthwellness.org. Accessed 2024.

Journal of EMDR Practice and Research. Edited by Jenny Ann Rydberg and Derek Farrell, vol. 17, no. 4, 2023, Springer Publishing. EMDR International Association, www.emdria.org.

The Journal of Personality and Social Psychology. Edited by Dolores Albarracin and Richard E. Lucas, American Psychological Association, ISSN 0022-3514.

Judith, Anodea. *Wheels of Life: A User's Guide to the Chakra System.* 1st ed., Llewellyn Publications, 2012.

Jung, Carl. *The Archetypes and the Collective Unconscious,* Princeton University Press, 1959.

Kabat-Zinn, Jon. *Full Catastrophe Living: Using the Wisdom of Your Body and Mind to Face Stress, Pain, and Illness.* Delta Trade Paperbacks, 1990.

Kehoe, Elizabeth, and Jonathan Egan. "Interpersonal Attachment Insecurity and Emotional Attachment to Possessions Partly Mediate the Relationship between Childhood Trauma and Hoarding Symptoms in a Non-clinical Sample." *Journal of Obsessive-Compulsive and Related Disorders,* vol. 21, 2019, pp. 37-45, doi:10.1016/j.jocrd.2018.12.001. Accessed 12 Jan. 1014.

Kiecolt-Glaser, Janice K., et al. "Omega-3 Fatty Acids, Oxidative Stress, and Leukocyte Telomere Length: A Randomized Controlled Trial." *Brain, Behavior, and Immunity,* vol. 28, 2013, pp. 16-24, doi:10.1016/j.bbi.2012.09.004. Accessed 13 Jan 2024.

Kohut, Heinz. *The Analysis of the Self: A Systematic Approach to the Psychoanalytic Treatment of Narcissistic Personality Disorders.* International Universities Press, 1971.

Kredentser, Maia S., Lesley A. Graff, and Charles N. Bernstein. "Psychological Comorbidity and Intervention in Inflammatory Bowel Disease." *Journal of Clinical Gastroenterology*, vol. 55, no. 1, Jan. 2021, pp. 30-35.

Levine, Peter A., and Maggie Kline. *Trauma Through a Child's Eyes: Awakening the Ordinary Miracle of Healing.* North Atlantic Books, 2007.

Neff, Kristin. *Self-Compassion: The Proven Power of Being Kind to Yourself,* William Morrow, 2011.

Novakovic, Vladan, et al. "Brain Stimulation in Posttraumatic Stress Disorder." *European Journal of Psychotraumatology*, vol. 2, no. 1, 2011, doi: 10.3402/ejpt.v2i0.5609

Pennebaker, James W. *Opening Up: The Healing Power of Expressing Emotions.* Guildford Press.

Romanowicz, M., et al. "A Case of a Four-Year-Old Child Adopted at Eight Months with Unusual Patterns and Significant Polypharmacy." *BMC Psychiatry*, vol. 17, 2017, p. 330. doi:10.1186/s12888-017-1492-y.

Rosenshine, Barak. "Study on Cognitive Engagement and Learning." *Journal of Educational Psychology.*

Schore, Allan N. "Attachment and the regulation of the right brain." *Attachment & Human Development*, vol. 2, no. 1, April 2000, pp. 23-47.

Striefel, S. "Creating the Future of Applied Psychophysiology and Biofeedback: From Fantasy to Reality." *Applied Psychophysiology and Biofeedback*, vol. 23, 1998, pp. 93-106, doi:10.1023/A:1022120506031

Substance Abuse and Mental Health Services Administration. "Adverse

Community Environments and Childhood Trauma." *Substance Abuse and Mental Health Services Administration*, 2014. www.samhsa.gov.

Szymanski, Kate, Linda Sapanski, and Francine Conway. "Trauma and ADHD: Association or Diagnostic Confusion? A Clinical Perspective." *Taylor & Francis Online*, Taylor & Francis, 2021, doi: 10.4324/978131770185-5.

Tarullo, Amanda R., and Megan R. Gunnar. "Child maltreatment and the developing HPA axis." *Hormones and Behavior*, vol. 50, no. 4, 2006, pp. 632-639.

Teahan, Patrick. "Was I Abused? Childhood PTSD Info and Questionnaire." YouTube, 2019, www.youtube.com.

Teicher, Martin H. "Impact of Childhood Trauma on Brain Development." *The Journal of Neuropsychiatry and Clinical Neurosciences*, 2024.

Van der Kolk, Bessel. *The Body Keeps the Score: Brain, Mind, and Body in the Healing of Trauma*. Penguin Books, 2015.

Van der Kolk, Bessel. "The Efficacy of Yoga in Treating PTSD Symptoms in Trauma Survivors." *Journal of Clinical Psychiatry*, vol. 35, no. 4, 2023, pp. 123-130.

Webb, Jonice. *Dr. Jonice Webb*. www.drjonicewebb.com. Accessed 2024.

Wheaton, Michael G., et al. "The Relationship between Anxiety Sensitivity and Obsessive-compulsive Symptom Dimentions." *Journal of Behavior Therapy and Experimental Psychiatry*, vol. 43, no. 3, 2012, pp. 891-896, www.doi.org/10.1016/j.jbtep.2012.01.001. Accessed January 2024.

White, Michael, and David Epston. "About Narrative Therapy Centre." *Narrative Therapy Centre*, narrativetherapycentre.com, Accessed Jan 2024.

Winnicott, D.W. *Essential Papers on Object Relations*. Edited by Peter Buckley, M.D., New York University, 1986.

FEELINGS WHEEL

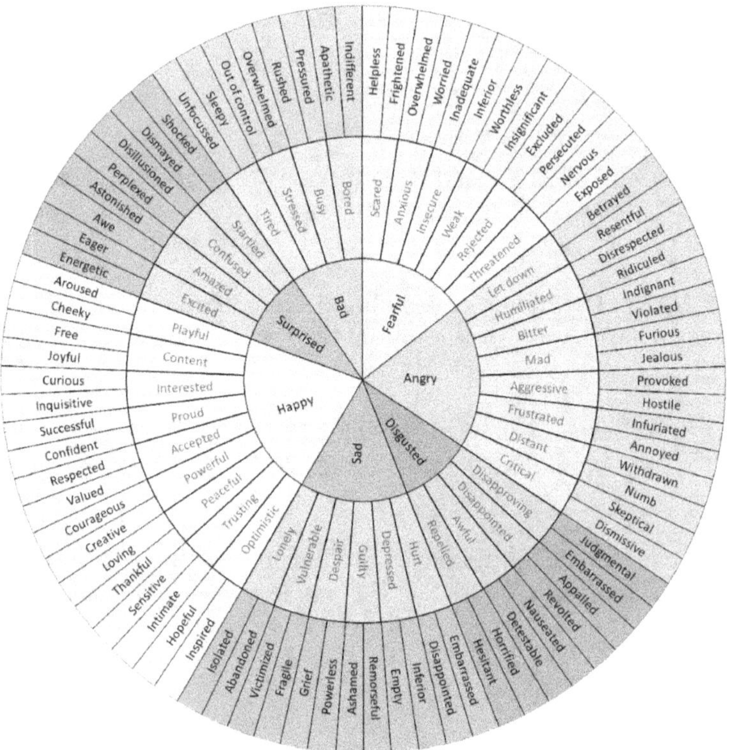

The Feelings Wheel is a visual tool that helps identify and articulate complex emotions. It consists of a central circle with core emotions, surrounded by concentric circles depicting related, more specific feelings.

How to Use: Start at the center with a basic emotion you're experiencing, like 'happy' or 'sad'. Then, move outward to the more nuanced emotions in the outer circles to better understand and describe your feelings. This tool aids in emotional awareness and communication.

CHILDHOOD TRAUMA ASSESSMENT CHECKLIST

Instructions: For each statement below, assign a score based on your experience during childhood:

0 = Never
1 = Rarely
2 = Sometimes
3 = Often
4 = Always

______ **Felt unsafe or threatened at home.**

______ **Witnessed or experienced physical abuse.**

______ **Suffered from emotional or verbal abuse.**

______ **Experienced neglect or lack of basic care.**

______ **Was pressured to take on adult responsibilities prematurely.**

______ **Endured bullying or severe teasing from peers or siblings.**

______ **Lived through significant family disruptions (divorce, death).**

______ **Witnessed or was exposed to substance abuse in the household.**

______ **Had to suppress emotions or aspects of my personality.**

______ **Was a victim of or exposed to sexual abuse or misconduct.**

______ **Lacked emotional support and understanding from caregivers.**

______ **Regularly faced criticism or lack of support from family.**

______ **Experienced traumatic events that were unaddressed**

______ **Felt isolated or struggled to make friends.**

______ **Grew up with a caregiver suffering from mental health issues.**

Comprehensive Healing Progress Tracker

Weekly Reflection

- Emotional State Check-In:
  - How have I been feeling this week? (e.g., anxious, calm, sad, happy)
  - What specific events or interactions influenced my emotional state?
- Therapy or Counseling Sessions:
  - What topics or issues did I discuss in therapy this week?
  - What insights or breakthroughs did I experience?
- Self-Care Practices:
  - What self-care activities did I engage in this week? (e.g., exercise, meditation, hobbies)
  - How did these activities impact my mood and overall well-being?
- Inner Child Work:
  - What specific exercises or practices did I use to connect with my inner child? (e.g., journaling, meditation, art)
  - What emotions or memories surfaced during these exercises?
- Relationship Dynamics:
  - How were my interactions with others this week? Were there any patterns I noticed?
  - How did my childhood experiences influence these interactions?
- Coping Strategies and Triggers:
  - What triggers did I encounter this week, and how did I respond?
  - Were there any new coping strategies that I tried? How effective were they?

- Adjustments and Flexibility: Remember to adjust this tracker as needed to fit your personal journey and experiences.
- Consistency and Patience: Aim for consistency in using this tracker, but be patient with yourself on days when it's challenging to reflect or document your experiences.

Comprehensive Healing Progress Tracker

Monthly Overview

- Overall Emotional Trends:
  - What were the predominant emotional trends over the month?
  - How do these compare to the previous month?
- Healing Milestones:
  - What significant milestones or progress in healing did I achieve this month?
  - How have my perspectives or feelings changed regarding my childhood experiences?
- Challenges and Growth Areas:
  - What challenges did I face this month in my healing journey?
  - What areas do I feel I need more growth or focus on?
- Support System Engagement:
  - How actively did I engage with my support system (therapist, support groups, friends)?
  - What role did this support play in my healing process this month?
- Physical Health and Wellness:
  - How was my overall physical health this month? (e.g., sleep, diet, exercise)
  - Did any physical changes correlate with my emotional state?

COMPREHENSIVE HEALING PROGRESS TRACKER

QUARTERLY REFLECTION

- Healing Journey Reflection:
  - Reflect on the past quarter – what were the major themes, insights, or growth areas in my healing journey?
  - How have my relationships and interactions evolved during this time?
- Goals and Aspirations:
  - What are my healing goals for the next quarter?
  - Are there new strategies or therapies I would like to explore?
- Self-Compassion and Acknowledgment:
  - How have I practiced self-compassion and acknowledged my progress?
  - In what ways can I further cultivate self-compassion in my healing journey?

YEARLY REVIEW

- Year in Review:
  - Reflect on the past year – what were the significant changes, challenges, and achievements in my healing journey?
  - How has my understanding and relationship with my inner child evolved?
- Lessons Learned:
  - What were the key lessons I learned about myself and my healing process?
  - How have these lessons shaped my approach to healing and personal growth?
- Future Outlook:
  - What are my long-term goals and aspirations for healing and growth?
  - How can I build on the progress made this year to continue my journey of healing?